I0016812

Mastering the Complex World of Software Management

Increasing Impact and Improving Performance for Software Managers

David J. Asher

Apress®

Mastering the Complex World of Software Management: Increasing Impact and Improving Performance for Software Managers

David J. Asher
Milford, MA, USA

ISBN-13 (pbk): 979-8-8688-0840-1   ISBN-13 (electronic): 979-8-8688-0841-8
https://doi.org/10.1007/979-8-8688-0841-8

Copyright © 2024 by David J. Asher

This work is subject to copyright. All rights are reserved by the Publisher, whether the whole or part of the material is concerned, specifically the rights of translation, reprinting, reuse of illustrations, recitation, broadcasting, reproduction on microfilms or in any other physical way, and transmission or information storage and retrieval, electronic adaptation, computer software, or by similar or dissimilar methodology now known or hereafter developed.

Trademarked names, logos, and images may appear in this book. Rather than use a trademark symbol with every occurrence of a trademarked name, logo, or image we use the names, logos, and images only in an editorial fashion and to the benefit of the trademark owner, with no intention of infringement of the trademark.

The use in this publication of trade names, trademarks, service marks, and similar terms, even if they are not identified as such, is not to be taken as an expression of opinion as to whether or not they are subject to proprietary rights.

While the advice and information in this book are believed to be true and accurate at the date of publication, neither the authors nor the editors nor the publisher can accept any legal responsibility for any errors or omissions that may be made. The publisher makes no warranty, express or implied, with respect to the material contained herein.

Managing Director, Apress Media LLC: Welmoed Spahr
Acquisitions Editor: Shivangi Ramachandran
Development Editor: James Markham
Project Manager: Jessica Vakili

Cover designed by eStudioCalamar

Distributed to the book trade worldwide by Apress Media, LLC, 1 New York Plaza, New York, NY 10004, U.S.A. Phone 1-800-SPRINGER, fax (201) 348-4505, e-mail orders-ny@springer-sbm.com, or visit www.springeronline.com. Apress Media, LLC is a California LLC and the sole member (owner) is Springer Science + Business Media Finance Inc (SSBM Finance Inc). SSBM Finance Inc is a **Delaware** corporation.

For information on translations, please e-mail booktranslations@springernature.com; for reprint, paperback, or audio rights, please e-mail bookpermissions@springernature.com.

Apress titles may be purchased in bulk for academic, corporate, or promotional use. eBook versions and licenses are also available for most titles. For more information, reference our Print and eBook Bulk Sales web page at http://www.apress.com/bulk-sales.

Any source code or other supplementary material referenced by the author in this book is available to readers on GitHub (https://github.com/Apress). For more detailed information, please visit https://www.apress.com/gp/services/source-code.

If disposing of this product, please recycle the paper

Table of Contents

TABLE OF CONTENTS

About the Author

David J. Asher brings an unusual perspective to software management based on his varied career as a product management leader, inventor, entrepreneur, systems analyst, and lifelong coder, in addition to leading engineering teams. Some of his roles were at well-known names like Amazon, Bose, Iron Mountain, Dialogic, Banyan Systems, and Grumman, while others were at smaller companies and startups. His software experience spans from cloud to mobile apps to firmware, and his backgrounds in physics, signal processing, sensors, and electronics further broaden his perspectives from pure software to complex real-time systems.

Asher developed a career pattern as an inside entrepreneur as he would work within companies to initiate and lead startup programs that result in disruptive new products. He authored multiple patents, published several mobile apps, and wrote the open-source software electron-firebase. His education includes an MBA from the University of New Hampshire, MS Electrical Engineering from SUNY Stony Brook, and BS in Physics and Computer Science from SUNY Albany. In his volunteer life, he is on the Board of Directors for a non-profit organization where he had served as VP and President, and serves on the Board of Advisors for the IT Management and Leadership (ITML) Institute.

ABOUT THE AUTHOR

Asher's career took an unusual twist. Transitioning from an Engineering Manager into a Product Manager is fairly common, but it is quite unusual to revert and rediscover engineering leadership and the joys of building teams that build great products. It is with all these experiences that he is now giving back to the community of software managers and challenging them to raise the bar on their leadership of technology development and people.

Acknowledgments

There is a whole aspect of becoming an effective manager that is neither technical nor business but that of being a good person and building trust and relationships with other people. This truly would not have developed in me without my wife, Dianne. I have told others that if they want to learn how to manage people they should have children, so thank you Miles and Seth for all of the management training you have given me! You have been an amazingly supportive family, especially during trying times of long work hours, distant travel, and recovering from layoffs. Special thanks to my mother for setting high expectations, to my father for putting a soldering iron in my hand, and to Ken Schwartz and Shane Bouslough for nearly a lifetime of sharing technology and music, work-life travails, friendship, and family.

The parade of talented managers and leaders that I have had the privilege to work with is uncountable, but through my career there have been a few stand-out mentors. Roughly in time sequence: Richie Simon (Sperry) for leading the team in my first career role as described in Chapter 2, "Career Foundations"; Ralph Waters (Photon Research) for showing the elegant management style of giving someone an impossible challenge, then stepping back; Joel Chadabe for our five-year wild ride together in Intelligent Music that ended cash-poor but experience-rich; Steve Davi (Banyan Systems) for suffering me as I was learning the craft of becoming an inside entrepreneur; George Kontopidis for not only hiring me into three companies (NMS Communications, Dialogic, Bose) but for being one of the few leaders I've witnessed that can show how to care for people and their careers while upholding the highest standards for engineering practice; John Potemri (NMS Communications, Bose)

ACKNOWLEDGMENTS

for showing how to make the social glue that keeps teams together and performing; John Nicol (NMS Communications, Bose) for even daring to make the attempt to turn me toward academia and so much more engineering stuff; Tom Mackowski and Mike Wipperfeld (Iron Mountain) for helping me fully develop into a product manager and internalize customer trust; Patrick Faucher and Dylan O'Mahoney (Bose) for running the experiment of zero-to-launch against all odds and proving the unmatched value of leading through partnership; and Eric Bloom as my muse in writing and publishing, non-profit governance, and family friends.

Introduction

It took me 40 years to write this book. What follows are my learnings in a career as a split-brained technology and business leader. This is my attempt to turn around and help others as they make their own career path of managing people and technology development.

TL;DR – The journey from individual contributor to manager to business leader is harder than you expect, and more rewarding than you imagine!

Each of the chapters has a focus that is mostly independent of the others, representing the many different dimensions of being a technical manager. The reader should feel free to jump to any chapters in the order that most draws their interest.

Who Can Benefit from This Book?

Building complex technology products and systems requires a team spanning many roles. Since this book takes a broad perspective, there are many career roles that can benefit.

- **Software developers** who are considering a management path for their career, or are feeling blocked by a lack of opportunity

- **Team tech leads** that are responsible for much of a software team's operation, whether they enter a management role or not

- **Software Development Managers** that want to improve their capabilities in order to take on more responsibilities, earn a promotion, or alter their career direction

- **Hardware Managers** that find themselves responsible for products and systems that contain a great deal of software but don't have an experience basis to manage it

- **Project Managers and Program Managers** that are considering people management or need to understand how better to work with Engineering Managers

- **Engineering directors and executives** that find themselves responsible for organizational success but may not be secure in their business training

- **Non-software technology leaders** because most of this material is directly applicable to technology development in general

- **Technology investors** to more fully understand some of the business and risk considerations when building complex software

- **Technology educators**, especially at graduate level, to better prepare students for technology management and people management roles

The management levels discussed in the following stop short of executive roles, in part because there is an industry of executive coaching and training that can be brought to bear when companies find value in it, and in part because my own executive experience is limited to startups and non-profit work.

Accumulated Experience in Technology and Business

Why should you trust the person offering this guidance? To answer, it would be helpful if I shared some of my background. As a career retrospective, I am breaking down my history into five-to-eight-year segments, which seem to mark major pivot points that launched me to new adventures and greater learning.

1979 to 1983 – Undergraduate

Education: BS, State University of New York at Albany, majors in Physics and Computer Science

Employment and Internship: University Photo Service; SUNY electronic music studio; Copytone photo printers; General Electric R&D Center

Roles: Chief Photographer; music lab assistant; darkroom technician; physics R&D intern, and I may have sold a few vacuum cleaners door-to-door

1983 to 1988 – US Defense Industry

Education: MS Electrical Engineering, State University of New York at Stony Brook, major in Signal Processing

Employment: Sperry Systems Management; Grumman Aerospace; Photon Research Associates

Projects: US Navy Command and Control System and Anti-Submarine Warfare for *Perry-class frigates*; CCS for Canada *Guided Missile Frigate*; US Navy *A6 Intruder* avionics and sensors upgrade; Strategic Defense Initiative *Boost Surveillance and Tracking System*

Roles: System analyst; algorithm developer

Independent Projects: Analog synthesizer (known as *The Duck*); completed a prototype MIDI controlled audio mixer at Digital Wave Technologies (startup)

1988 to 1993 – Intelligent Music

Employment: Intelligent Music (startup).

Projects: *TouchSurface* pressure-sensitive low-cost touch sensor for musical instruments and pointing device for laptops

Roles: Inventor and patent writing, touch sensor designer, screen-print manufacturing technician, analog circuit engineer, embedded controller hardware and firmware engineer, device driver coder, demonstration app coder, low volume product assembler, marketing, selling, fundraising, board member

Personal: Moved to upstate New York; met and married my life partner, Dianne

1993 to 1999 – Enterprise System Software

Education: Executive MBA, University of New Hampshire

Employment: SystemSoft; Banyan Systems; Lewtan Technologies

Projects: Laptop BIOS firmware development; Network Operating System (Banyan VINES) client development; *Banyan Intranet Connect* web service for corporate email access over the Internet; *ABS-Net* website for subscription access to Asset-Backed Securities deal information

Roles: BIOS developer; network O/S engineer; tech lead; software manager

Personal: Moved to Massachusetts; two children born – Miles and Seth

2000 to 2007 – Telecom Equipment

Employment: NMS Communications (f.k.a. Natural Microsystems)

Projects: High density media processing telecom components and system software; system conversion to Linux; *Vision Media Server* for rapid building of interactive voice and video mobile applications over cellular networks

Roles: Engineering Manager for O/S and Drivers; Director of Engineering Operations; Pro Services Manager; Director of Product Management

Independent Projects: Theremin-1 using classic radio antenna configuration and transistors for sensing and direct sound generation

2007 to 2015 – Cloud Storage and Mobile Apps

Employment: Iron Mountain Digital; Self-employed DBA Mapocosm; Dialogic, ViziApps (startup)

Projects: *LiveVault* online backup for servers; *Connected* online backup for personal computers; *CloudRecovery* joint product development with Microsoft Data Protector; *Freedom Trail Boston* mobile app for iPhone and Android (and other mobile app experiments); *ViziApps* low-code rapid development platform for mobile apps

Roles: Director of Product Management; independent app writer and publisher; VP Product

Independent Projects: Theremin-2 using Arduino, ultrasonic ranging sensors, and 8-bit software FM sound generator

2015 to 2023 – Internet-of-Things and Cloud

Employment: Bose; Amazon Web Services

Projects: Bose *Galapagos* internal Cloud and IoT platform for consumer audio devices (media streaming and speech-enabled); AWS File Gateway for shuttling enterprise data to Amazon S3 cloud storage

Roles: Head of Cloud IoT Platform; Software Development Manager

Independent Projects: Theremin-3 using ESP32, laser ranging sensors, and 24-bit software FM sound generator; *electron-firebase* open-source software for quick-start building of cloud-connected cross-platform desktop apps

Volunteering: Five-year VP and President cycle for non-profit organization

Just a note about my past employers and the divisions that employed me: for those keeping score, you may notice that most of them no longer exist as the entities they were. Technology development is a rough and dynamic business.

Terminology and Stuff

This book generally focuses on the development of software, but much of the content can be applied to other forms of technology development. This is especially true for complex products and systems that mix software within hardware design and manufacturing programs. Pretty much all references to "software" can be interpreted in the broadest sense of not only code but specifications, quality assurance, documentation, security, technical support, operations, methodologies – just about any and all aspects of software ideation, creation, operation, and maintenance.

Terms like Software Manager, Engineering Manager, and several variations are almost always used interchangeably. These are capitalized to denote well-established and widely understood roles in the technology industries. Generally in tech companies, a director is a manager that has managers on their staff, and a VP is a manager that has directors on their staff. This book doesn't make distinctions and uses the term "manager" to apply to all of these levels of management.

None of the technical definitions herein have been copied from other sources, including definitions of intellectual property, business, and accounting terms. These all come from my experience and understanding of the topics, expressed in ways that I believe are useful to any Engineering Manager. Lawyers and accountants may quibble with the precision of some of these definitions, but they are not plagiarized or overloaded with unfamiliar jargon.

I have used many personal stories throughout this book so that abstract concepts are reduced to real examples. These are all accurate to the best of my memory. In some stories I have used first names of people to help personalize the narrative, though these names may or may not reflect the actual people involved.

My hope for you is to learn how to capture surprising opportunities, create opportunities when they seem scarce, elevate your appreciation of management and business to the same level that you have mastered bits and bolts, and have fun and be happy while building great technology.

CHAPTER 1

Call to Action

Are you ready to lead? As Steve Jobs noted: "You know who the best managers are? They're the great individual contributors who never ever want to be a manager, but decide they have to be a manager, because no one else is going to be able to do as good a job as them."

I have witnessed many capable technology leaders make terrible business blunders, and likewise for capable business leaders making terrible technology blunders. These leaders failed to appreciate how difficult problems are outside of their expertise. Such failures come from our personal blind spots of being confident in our mastery over one domain, and then presume we must be good in others. If I'm already successful, can it really be so difficult? Even worse is the hubris of making decisions based on intuition when evidence can be available. Markets are not kind to these behaviors.

I have not seen business leaders become masters of technology; success in a technology business doesn't seem to work in this direction. So our call to action is for technology leaders to expand their skills and perspective into management and business realms. This may be hard, but it is possible, and the starting point is appreciating that business problems are every bit as challenging and nuanced as technology problems. It takes training, mentoring, and experience to become that master – anything less and you're just making things up.

© David J. Asher 2024
D. J. Asher, *Mastering the Complex World of Software Management*,
https://doi.org/10.1007/979-8-8688-0841-8_1

Bear Markets

Technology companies have been playing casino games when it comes to developing management talent and business leaders. We promote a lot of people to be managers and then promote some of those managers toward greater levels of responsibility, such that the best ones filter up through the organizational hierarchy. The outcome is not what we think: this random process is effective at filling slots; it is not designed to produce the best leaders.

Do you know the saying: "You can't tell the difference between a brilliant investment strategy and a bull market"? The dynamics of technology companies work this way, too. When you are an emerging tech company that is growing gangbusters and investors are throwing cash at you and customers are lining up for your product, it seems you can do little wrong and all of the managers are brilliant.

Except – that phase of tech company growth is like a bull market. It is when competition goes on the attack and the economy tanks and new technologies threaten your position – a technology bear market – that you find out who are the really good managers. If you've been lucky enough to keep them. Companies that don't train managers to deal with adversities such as the coming bear market, and it always comes, won't get to keep their success.

Career Diversity

My father was an electrical engineer and Engineering Manager for a single company from before college graduation to retirement, and he found my early career choices to be perplexing. I knew for sure that the kind of quid pro quo corporate loyalty he took for granted would not apply to my generation, and somehow I sensed headwinds that informed me to build personal resiliency through diverse learning and experiences.

That attitude ultimately led me through a career that crossed many industries, spanning software and hardware products, large cloud systems and operations, product management and engineering management, continual pursuit of innovation, and entrepreneurship.

This book will assume a very broad perspective because of these diverse career experiences, which is fitting for the wildly varied and unexpected jobs often thrown to an Engineering Manager. As we build ever more complex and highly integrated products and systems, it is incumbent on Engineering Managers to master multiple technical disciplines as well as all of the people management and business leadership demanded from senior responsibility roles.

In repeatedly shifting my role, I have enjoyed the benefit of a great many role models and mentors. They have been essential to my professional growth and shown what works well and sometimes what is less effective. There just isn't enough thanks in the world for them all, except to pay it forward. So here we go.

Off the Happy Path

Software developers often talk about a happy path, the ideal sequence of code that falls neatly within the intended design of a product or system. It is the easiest code to write and test because nothing goes wrong, users do nothing surprising, all inputs are well inside of expected boundaries, and there are no serious errors. It is life without friction. All is happy.

Talking about a happy path is useful because that enables us to agree on the main purpose of the software we are building, and the first thing that you want to test is the happy path to show that the primary value of your software is being delivered. However, if you construct code only for the happy path it would be brittle because - in the real world - exceptions happen all the time. Software only becomes reliable and trusted after it has been continuously improved through many encounters off the happy path.

3

Defining goals for your career is like following a happy path, but you can't thrive on a happy path because life's exceptions are unrelenting. Twists and turns seem greater for management roles than for individual contributors, and even more so for the tumultuous world of technology development than many other occupations. Being prepared to wander off the happy path will help you to build a successful and enjoyable career.

I cannot give you a prescription for success in technology management. One size won't fit all, and travels off the happy path for one person will be different than for everyone else. Rather, I am attempting to share my diversity of learning that comes from changing my perspective, in large ways every few years, and in small ways almost continually.

Risk and Reward

How often should you veer off your happy path and make job changes, and how big should they be? When should you accept an unexpected assignment from your employer, or pursue one? My rule of thumb is based on comfort level: if I feel myself getting too comfortable, if my learning has slowed, and if work is starting to seem more routine than exciting, then I start itching for a change. It's a highly personal question as many people gravitate toward stability and familiarity, but non-action presents a risk of its own.

In my early career, the main considerations for jumping to a new employer were mostly about salary, advancement, interesting work, benefits like health insurance and tuition reimbursement, and maybe some contextual factors like location, commute, and office environment. Also, there is sometimes the issue of getting away from a boss that is making your life miserable, which is something I hadn't experienced but some people do.

As tech companies increasingly moved compensation to stock options, stock purchase plans, and restricted stock units, equity vesting became an important factor because leaving a job could result in sacrificing a substantial future payout. And if you are joining a startup, there could be a long-term commitment required in order to get a big compensation upside through an acquisition or public offering.

All of this means that changing your role or job isn't just a straightforward consideration about salary and work, but a more complex set of risk and reward trade-offs that most of us engineers aren't financially literate enough to analyze. Even if you are forced into a career transition because of a layoff, as I have been several times, bouncing back will require a lot of work and a fresh set of decisions about new opportunities and how to evaluate them.

It is the reward that motivates us, and the risks that hold us back. As with coding, it is helpful to consider any career decisions with a vision for your own happy path.

Leap into Incompetence

It may be tempting to now consider the Peter Principle, referring to research and a book by Laurence J. Peter, simply expressed as "In a hierarchy, every employee tends to rise to his level of incompetence." There is a dark, satirical aspect to this work that forebodes the executive ranks of companies staffed with bumbling incompetence. Since my own observations inform me that great companies can't have become great through bumbling, there must be something else at play.

Think about a career juncture, whether it is taking a new assignment, or a new role, or a promotion, or switching into a different industry or technical discipline. It is the very novelty of it that ensures there will be unfamiliar aspects where you have not yet built competence. We enter every new job with a certain level of incompetence, and our success depends on identifying our incompetencies and overcoming them. It's your competence that convinces people to take a leap of faith that you can succeed in a new role, and it's your incompetence that presents risks that you may not.

We really don't want others to see our incompetencies, so we try to project ourselves as having greater competence than we may possess. Some say that we "fake it till we make it," and some internalize the feeling as "imposter syndrome." So let's get this straight, overcoming our own incompetencies is a totally normal – even essential – aspect of building a career that advances in responsibility. Don't let your own incompetence get in the way of taking on a new challenge.

Recap

If you find yourself getting frustrated at the decisions and actions of managers in your company, then it's time to step up. But being a fantastic engineer and believing in yourself isn't good enough; after all, that's how those managers got promoted, so why would you be any better? Your path to success, and actually having better outcomes than those people that you criticize, starts with appreciating the wide-ranging skills and understandings needed to be an effective Engineering Manager.

CHAPTER 2

Career Foundations

Ascending to a career in Software Management or any kind of Technology Management presumes that you have been competent as an engineer. Along the way you will encounter many choices that make it more or less likely that you might have the opportunity to become a manager and succeed at it. The career path will be different for every one of us, but there are some foundations that can help you on your journey.

Kickstarting a Career

As I entered college, one thing I knew with absolute certainty was that my career path would be an academic life in physics research. Based on no information whatsoever, I surmised that the greatest tool ever invented for physics research was just becoming widely available – the computer – and that if I learned how to write programs, I could enjoy a special career advantage. So this was my 100% certain goal to guide my education and career.

My first lucky break was attending a college that had no liberal arts requirements, which enabled me to design a course of study combining physics and computer science, and complete two unrelated technical majors in four years. It turns out that learning physics was perfect preparation to becoming a top-notch coder, since physicists are trained to start with an answer and then figure out the problem setup and path to solution. CS programs tend to miss this deep problem-solving aspect of coding craft. Physics is also an exercise in understanding how the

© David J. Asher 2024
D. J. Asher, *Mastering the Complex World of Software Management*,
https://doi.org/10.1007/979-8-8688-0841-8_2

world works and teasing out the most subtle principles from confusing observations. Once you can decode nature in this way, you build confidence to work through all sorts of messy man-made problems.

My second lucky break was a summer internship at the GE corporate R&D facility leading into my senior year. Four of us were selected by a physics professor, and I'm sure my background in programming was a big factor. While the scientists at GE were a fantastic bunch, I realized that the pace of work in the physics realm would be measured in years and decades, whereas my internal clock rate for building things and seeing results is measured in months if not days. Total mismatch. I had to admit that physics wouldn't work for me as a career.

My third lucky break was graduating into the severe jobs recession of 1982–1983. Huh? It was a tough environment to launch a career for all of my friends and classmates. I landed a job at a defense contractor and the reason was the same for many of my co-workers that also shared a last name with a more senior employee. That's how it worked. But this quickly forced me into a software engineering career path, which was exactly what I needed.

Goal Setting

You will notice that, even as early as leaving high school, I had established a career goal, and in fact a lifestyle goal, with perfect vision and clarity. And then it took me more than three years of college to realize how wrong I was and another year to figure out how to start making corrections in my goal. Was it wrong to set a goal that turned out to be incorrect? I say, "no." With a goal, you are moving in a direction, learning things with a purpose, and opening doors of opportunity. Without a goal, you are leaving opportunities to chance, at best.

While I was trying to sort this out, my mother presented me with a news clipping, which I read and responded to dismissively, "Yeah I know about this company making a BASIC compiler. Yuk. No, I'm thinking about the ways that computers can be embedded into devices and using software to make them smart. And anyway, you want me to move to Seattle??"

I was right about this new goal, enjoying many years of embedded systems development in all sorts of products and industries, later moving to Web technologies and the Cloud, where this eventually all collided into the Internet of Things. So this new career goal definitely worked well for me, but I also have to admit completely missing the early signal my mother offered about Microsoft and the changes the Personal Computer was about to unleash on the world.

It turns out that this first job out of college into a US defense contractor, and especially my first boss, offered some experiences that turned into foundational lessons, so I'll share these stories and maybe the lessons can help in guiding your career, too. Our shared goal, you and me, is to become better managers for our engineering teams and organizations.

Not Coding

As soon as I started this new job in the world of software engineering for defense systems, I asked my boss, "Do you have any work that isn't coding?" What a silly and precocious question. What was I thinking? Well, the kinds of coding assignments at college weren't that interesting and I was hoping there was some greater challenge awaiting me than coding. I guess it hadn't occurred to me that coding real world projects could be immensely interesting and challenging. Yet, I had no idea what a non-coding assignment in a software team could possibly be. Maybe my boss saw a connection with our shared background in physics, but he took the bait and told me to join the Systems Analysts.

A Systems Analyst functions something like a Product Manager: thoroughly understanding customer requirements, ensuring that engineers correctly translate requirements into a design, guiding the implementation to keep development on track and make corrections, and evaluating the results through testing. It's kind of ridiculous for an entry-level software engineer to walk into a systems analyst role, since you need to know a lot and I didn't know anything.

The systems analysts on the team carried a career of wisdom and experience, so this was a fabulous mentoring opportunity and I went into sponge mode, trying to understand as much as I could and add value at any turn. I have no regrets about avoiding coding in this first job, because this was such a wonderful assignment.

This lesson is to sometimes swerve out of your lane. In this case, it was with my eyes shut and just pulling the wheel. There will be risks when you swerve, it will be uncomfortable, but always driving within your lane carries its own risks over the long term, like not making satisfying progress in your career.

Team Productivity

My boss didn't exhibit many knick-knacks, but he did have a graph tacked to the wall by his desk that looked something like Figure 2-1.

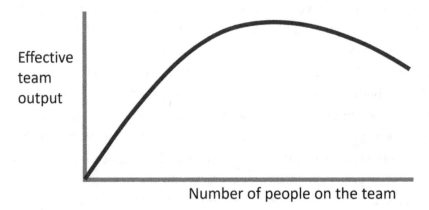

Figure 2-1. *Team productivity curve*

I can't recall who made this study and we can certainly question what kind of methodology would lead to such a finding that we might want to trust. No matter, let's look at the principle.

Zero is easy: no output if no one is on the team. One is easy: one person has an effective output of themselves. Then when you have two people on the team, don't you get double the effective output of one person? You don't. If those two people were perfectly decoupled and working on independent assignments, then you would get twice the output of one, but the whole point is that they are on a team and therefore must coordinate their work because they have a shared mission. They must communicate to each other, and sometimes negotiate, and sometimes work out disagreements. Little issues that one person can figure out alone, in their head, become "overhead" as soon as two people are involved.

Now consider three people on the team. With only two people there was just one interpersonal connection between them. Just by adding one person, now we have three interpersonal connections – we tripled the overhead! And with four people on the team, there would be six interpersonal connections. Figure 2-2 shows what this growth looks like. The overhead, based on interpersonal connections, is growing exponentially with the number of people on the team. Actually, the growth in overhead cost is $n(n-1)/2$. How could a team ever possibly get any real work done with all of that overhead cost? And how can you possibly manage team growth as this pernicious runaway problem is chewing up all of your productive time?

Figure 2-2. *Communication overhead growth*

This is the whole point of managing software development as a team. If things are disorganized, if people are unclear about their goals, if some people are underperforming and need to keep bothering others for help, if the deliverable definition keeps changing, if important processes aren't documented, if, if, if. There are so many factors that can drive up team overhead and grind a team's pace to a maddeningly slow and unprofitable outcome.

This is one of the most critical functions of a Software Manager – identify and reduce as many of the overhead factors as possible so that the team has a realistic chance of meeting their deliverable goals.

Take Notes

One day my boss said to me, "grab a pencil and paper and join me for this meeting, I want you to take notes." I asked what he was expecting me to capture for the notes, and he said, "it doesn't matter what happens in the meeting, what matters is what you write in your notes and give to others." I'm sure your first reaction is, "how cynical," and then your second reaction is, "how true."

When you have a meeting, or even a discussion with just another person, and you have come to some agreement, don't think that the decision is done and committed. Even with the best of intentions for all parties to keep to a shared commitment – and best intentions is not always the case – people have different perspectives and will interpret things differently, especially in the details. The way to confirm that everyone is actually in agreement is to write it down and ask others for confirmation. We don't need legal contracts for all of the little things that we discuss and agree to, but we do need to make sure that we are agreeing to the same thing.

Writing is the best way, really the only way, to make sure that multiple parties are in agreement. Writing also enables communication to parties that weren't involved in the discussion. You may think that, as an engineer, all of your work is technical, all numbers and code, and please leave writing for the English majors. Wrong. Writing is core to your job.

We cannot build successful products without achieving complete alignment on our goals, designs, implementations, tests, and even our inventions and our dreams. All of this demands that you be a good writer. Being a "good writer" in the engineering world, and in the business world more generally, means economical and clear communication. It's not creative writing and definitely not fiction. In fact, I've sometimes advised engineering students to take a journalism class, which is much more akin to the kind of communication that we need.

And if you are the one doing the writing, you get the privilege of having commitments told from your perspective. That's awesome power, please use it wisely.

Be Helpful

Trustworthy. Loyal. Helpful. Friendly. Courteous. Kind. Obedient. Cheerful. Thrifty. Brave. Clean. Reverent. Yep, I'm an Eagle Scout, and these rules for leadership learned at a young age aren't just sticky, but a great foundation for a career. Let's look at #3, being helpful.

Our team was writing the command and control software for a class of US Navy frigates. There were many software modules with a message-passing facility for the modules to communicate, and I had trouble getting my head around the system as a whole. It seemed to me that the key to understanding the system was in the way the modules communicate, but there was no such guide. So I walked through every module, collecting all of the messages into one binder so that I can see the whole in one place, from a communications perspective. The process enabled me to absorb more of the system's inter-workings. Then the binder went on the shelf as a quick reference for future troubleshooting and consulting to help the other engineers with their work.

In order to determine our team's performance on the contract and even our profitability, we had to pass a review which happened just a few months later. It was common for the US and Australian navies to cooperate in many areas, so our reviewer happened to be an Australian, whom I'll refer to as Commander Smith. Being a systems analyst, I was in the room during the review, but was just observing and didn't make a squeak. Things were going very well for us, maybe too well. It's a reviewer's job to find problems after all, otherwise how else would you know that they were seriously reviewing? And Commander Smith was starting to get a little frustrated since our cracker-jack team only left little crumbs to find.

Towards the end of the performance review, Commander Smith read out one of the last items he needed to check: "Intermodule Message Specification." Blank stares all around. "Haven't you got an Intermodule Message Specification?" Blank stares all around. He grinned and waved his pen with a bit of glee and a chuckle as he went to mark this one glaring error. I was wondering what this missing document was, and was thinking that I hadn't seen one, and what could it be, but oh didn't I put together something like that a few months ago?

At this point, reflexes took over and I'm sure I stopped thinking altogether as I jumped up and yelled "Wait, I've Got It!" Then sprinted out of the room, down the hall, over to my bookshelf, oh there it is, grabbed the binder, huffed back to the meeting, burst back into the conference room, and placed my binder on the table right in front of Commander Smith.

He picked it up, leafed through a few pages, looked at the spine, and read out "Intermodule Message Specification," verbatim what he was asking for. Then in his best Aussie, declared as he ran his finger along the spine, "Looks like the ink hasn't dried on this one yet, has it, mate?" The moment was at once heroic, deeply embarrassing, and hysterically funny.

We did quite well on our performance review since we delivered the goods, and the last piece came together because several months prior I was just trying to be helpful and organize things a bit. And this is the best advice that I can offer to any engineer – how to stand out, how to improve, how to advance? Be proactive, find things that need fixing, and help others.

How Big?

Our company was awarded a contract to design and build a new class of ships for the Canadian Navy. My team wasn't directly involved in this; however, my boss was, and he pulled me into an early program definition effort. I was splitting my time between the home team in New York and a newly forming team in Montreal, helping to get this program launched.

One day our home team went out for dinner at a Chinese restaurant. The group was having a good laugh at my situation, saying "pack your bags!" and predicting I would soon be called to move to Montreal to work full time on the new program. As dinner ended, we passed around the fortune cookies. I cracked mine, and passed the fortune to a coworker because I was too shocked to read it aloud. It said: "You need a new environment. Try Canada."

I swear this is exactly what happened, down to the letter. Never before or since in the world history of cookies has a fortune like this been found. So you are predicting that cookie presaged my move to Montreal and a completely new career and life direction, but that did not happen. My apologies to the fortune writer. You can see, though, that sometimes your career presents an opportunity that could drastically change your life direction, even your fortune. You may work hard to enable these opportunities, but it is not always right to take them. Just don't carry regrets, it's better to put your energy and emotion toward making the next opportunity.

It played out differently for my boss, though. He ended up with a sweet VP position in a new company formed to service this contract, and indeed he moved to Montreal. One of the engineers on the team approached him and dished out some sarcasm at his success, "You're a bigger mess-up than I am, how did you end up with the VP spot?" Our boss grinned, cupped his hands together like holding two grapefruits, and said, "They have to be this big!"

This is a most important lesson: there is no magic, rarely is there luck, and no one else will manage your career. You need to find or make opportunities, and grab them when it's right.

Being Organized

Organized, not as in arranging things to work better, but as in trade union. This first job was in a union shop and I was a member of the International Brotherhood of Electrical Workers. New York is a closed union state, meaning that paying union dues is compulsory. This seems highly unusual for software engineers, but software was just a small adjunct compared to all the workers building ships and missiles and computers and other defense hardware.

After a couple of years in this role, I could see there were rumblings and meetings about the upcoming contract and union members weren't satisfied. I attended a meeting, curious to see what the issues were about, and they were all about retirement benefits – health care and pension. One of the systems analysts from our team, although getting closer to retirement himself, got up to speak: "What are we doing about the young generation? What about tuition and other benefits that will attract them? How will this company keep going without bringing in fresh talent?" What unselfish and far-sighted comments. And of course they were met with cheers of "Sit down and shut up!" Ugh.

We went on strike for three weeks, and we were all assigned picket duty on the line. As I mentioned the nepotism rampant in these companies at the time, this also set up situations where one family member was striking and often a parent or other close relative was in management and crossing the picket line. Awkward.

I walked away from this experience understanding that there could be conflicts of interest between management and workers, and although I fully support worker's rights to unionize, I also recognized what an imperfect solution trade unions are, at least in the way that it's practiced in America. In part because, like our legal system, they are set up to be confrontational rather than cooperating to arrive at compromise positions.

But the bigger lesson for me is that the presence of a trade union is a symptom of management weaknesses that often happen with or without a union. We fail to understand employee values and situations, fail to act with a modicum of generosity, and fail to share information and communicate clearly. Don't let yourself be one of those managers contributing to such failures. It's hard work to build a healthy culture and professional relationships, but that is way better than the alternative of distrust and decay.

Nail Clippings

This first job was good work, good pay, and a great team, so people weren't leaving on their own. I only recall one engineer getting transferred out of the team. Unlike most every other engineer on the team, I didn't really interact with him and couldn't figure out what work he was doing there. But after all this was a union shop and it probably took quite a bit of management effort to displace an underperformer. One day, his chair was empty. We looked to clean out his desk, opened the desk drawer, and found one of the pencil tray cups filled with nail clippings. Yuk.

Now I know what he was doing. But that yuk has been a much more powerful metaphor than the classic "cobwebs" growing on someone because they don't move.

Here's the choice that you have in your career: you can move on your terms and your initiative, or you can let others move you. Moving is learning. Moving is being challenged. Moving is volunteering. Moving is building relationships. Moving is taking unfamiliar and risky assignments. Moving is being sensitive to your own comfort and realizing when you've been too comfortable for too long. Move or be moved.

Stop Fixing Things

I want to share just one other foundational career and life lesson, which didn't happen to come from my first job, but it was so helpful to me. This happened during my study in an MBA program, and of course any business school collects people from a wide swath of backgrounds and careers. Within this diverse group, I'm sure it wasn't hard to spot me as an engineer (because, you know, come on).

Deb was another student in our MBA program, and one day we were chatting. She was married to an engineer, and a recent exchange must have been fresh on her mind and hard to escape. Deb tells me that she and her husband were talking, and she got so frustrated that she blurted this out: "Stop fixing things! I don't need you to solve everything that I tell you. Sometimes, I just need you to listen, I - just - need - you - to - listen!" Oh. Ohhhhhhh.

Opportunity Knocks

Let's say that you set your sights on a management career, or any other advancement goal involving a change in your role. Three things have to align: you must want it, your skills must be a close match, and an opportunity must present itself. The first two are all about your personal training and ambitions; they are about being prepared. As you journey through your career, the aspect of opportunity is something you should be considering and have your antennae up to sense for it, because you can't control the timing of it.

You may think that you would be fantastic as a manager and already possess the needed skills, but that means nothing in your current situation if there is no opportunity. Companies do not create a role just to satisfy a worker's need for advancement and role change – just the opposite, a need arises because of growth or reorganization or someone is leaving their role and the spot needs to be filled. So there is an element of timing and luck for such career shifts to happen – you being in the right place at the right time with the right skills.

If you are feeling great pressure to change your role, perhaps because you are stagnating in your current role or some other factor, then you have a choice. You can patiently wait for an opportunity, or be proactive in searching for a new role outside of your team.

Opportunity tends to knock on your door in one of three ways: a position opens in your company that seems to be a good match for you; someone you know in another team or company, such as a former manager, calls you to fill their need; or a recruiter finds you and thinks you'll be a good match for a position they are hiring for. In all of these situations, you have no control over timing and possibility, other than to increase the likelihood of being asked by always being helpful to others, trying to work on assignments that lead to noticeable achievements, and keep nurturing your professional relationships and connections.

When a management opportunity knocks on your door and you are not inclined to pursue it, you should first consider the consequences before giving your answer. This opportunity may not knock again, so you may want to seriously consider it even if you feel unprepared. We are all unprepared to enter management. You may have a preconception about management, or perceive just the hassle of it without understanding the joys and satisfaction, so check your bias by asking a few managers about their experiences. Then there is also a risk that you may find yourself reporting to someone new, and this relationship may not result in a positive outcome for you. But you can't complain about the lack of opportunities if you refused to take a management offer when it presented itself.

Opportunity Squirms

There is a kind of reverse opportunity that you may encounter, which is that an opportunity presents itself but someone else is selected for the role. It may be a coworker, even a friend, or it could be someone brought in from another team or outside the company. This could be very frustrating – *hey, what about me?* But think about your role from the company's perspective. You are excellent and very valuable in what you do, but this new opportunity is about what you *do not* do, so how would your company know to envision you taking on an unproven role?

This kind of corporate short-sightedness about challenging people to grow is extremely common and has more to do with risk – a manager assumes less risk bringing in someone who has already proven themselves in a similar role, even if that person is not familiar. At least they reason that is the case. Since such opportunities may not come along very often, it can truly hurt your career if you miss out on a promotion in this way. So if you have a vision of a different role for yourself, it's important to have career planning discussions with your manager so they can help in finding opportunities and guiding them your way. They can't read your mind, so you need to tell them.

There is no shame in leaving a team or company to advance your own interests. However, if you are making critical contributions to some milestone, or possess some intellectual property that hasn't been well shared with others, it is in your own best interests to manage the timing so that you don't cause undue frustration and overwork to the colleagues that you are leaving behind.

This is about reputation. As you move through your career, you will be astounded at how many people you meet from earlier experiences. You know the expression, "never burn a bridge"? It applies perfectly to your career. You will run into people that you know in future roles, so make sure that if you do leave a position, even if you are frustrated, you continue to be a good team player and be helpful and kind to your colleagues. Building an outstanding reputation is one of the best ways for opportunities to find you.

Avoiding Management

The rest of this book will consider many aspects of managing software development, but are you considering all of your options when you make a career shift into management? Let's look at some of the roles and career tracks that can keep you close to hands-on engineering but not managing people, which may be just the right thing for you. Many of these start with an engineering foundation. For sure, you will at least need to work with many people in these roles, and from time to time you may need to hire them. I have often heard engineers and even managers speak confusingly about project managers and program managers and product managers – *what do they do, anyway?* So let's also clear up some of this confusion.

Much of this book has a gravity toward product development engineering – the people that write the code to build the many products that we use, but in the following we can see how many different roles are required to pull this off. Please accept my apologies for any important roles that I may have missed. Now, presented in no particular order.

Architect: Some small percentage of engineers are titled as "architect" or function as an architect. In software, they create the highest-level organization of a system so that multiple teams can tackle different aspects of a design problem resulting in major pieces coming together to work harmoniously. Mistakes made at this architectural level have an enormous impact on the rest of a project's cost and quality, whereas clever approaches could create a sustained competitive advantage that lead to real financial gains. Architects also guide the whole development process to promote adherence to the agreed-upon architecture, and investigate unanticipated problems that challenge the architecture and need robust solutions. The best architects are naturally mentors and code reviewers, helping younger engineers to develop critical skills. I have seen companies expect engineers to be trained or to eventually be promoted to an architect role; however, in my experience, a few engineers are naturally architects and show their capabilities as system-level thinkers by the time they are 25, else it may be unrealistic to expect others to become very effective at it.

Fellow: There could be other names for it, but this role rewards an engineer that enjoyed a highly productive and influential career with a position equivalent in stature and compensation to a non-executive senior manager. In a complex company with multiple programs and lines of business, a Fellow may not be assigned to any one project, but helps guide top-level product strategy and coordinates technology and resources between programs. Sometimes an "office of the CTO" may be a natural place for this level of accomplished engineer. The occurrence of this position, if it even exists in your company, is well below 1% of the population, so it is also a bit risky to plan a career goal based on achieving a Fellow position.

Tech Lead: As a team grows, it becomes harder for the team's manager to be deeply involved in all technical aspects, so a gap forms between the need for engineers to be guided, and their manager's time and capabilities. A Tech Lead can satisfy this gap. They are an engineer, typically more senior, but willing and interested to dive deeply into the technical implementations of each team member, and work closely with them to make sure they understand their assignment, aren't getting stuck on a technical or procedural problem, are delivering with the expected level of quality, and are faithfully reporting their progress. Some teams have a more formalized Tech Lead position for a length of time or duration of a project, but I find that it's also a good idea to challenge people to take team lead assignments and rotate the Tech Lead role. I have found some mature engineers to respond, when I ask them if they would consider management, with "no way!!" Taking a Tech Lead role may be a great way to have influence and responsibility without shifting your career into management.

Quality Engineer: Coders must always take responsibility for the quality of their work, which means testing their own code as it is developed. But who takes responsibility for the overall quality of a large project, especially the system-level and integration-level aspects that don't seem to fall on any one engineer's plate? While a coding engineer (or several) could be assigned this responsibility, there are other factors to consider. One is too much familiarity, because it is just very difficult for an engineer to change their mindset to work at a systemic level when their attention has been deep in the details. Another is their approach to thinking. Quality engineers tend to be able to see a system, not just holistically, but from many failure modes that development engineers often don't have the aptitude and training to tease out. Coders can be fantastic at this role, especially if they bring a spirit of automation, but they need to adjust.

Infrastructure Engineer: You have hopefully heard the expression "infrastructure as code." All of the things where we used to have systems administrators build and document how they did it are now best done in code so they are perfectly repeatable and completely documented. Plus so much more as this practice now extends to build and delivery processes, cloud systems, testing, monitoring, upgrades, and just about anything relating to building and running code in the world. Automate everything; it's coding but about operations and infrastructure. Especially as systems grow this field has its own unique complexities and challenges.

Network Engineer: Most coders know the basics of networking and can be effective at building networked applications, in large measure because most applications and services are relying upon layers of libraries and sub-services to take care of the hard stuff. But when things get a little more complicated or when subtle problems arise, they may fall back on their scant understanding and make assumptions that just aren't true. I've seen this pattern too often, and it sometimes leads to very bad results. It takes many years of learning and experience to truly understand how networks operate, how protocols behave, how performance degrades, and many other fine points. Therefore, we need network engineers.

Security Engineer: It's a dangerous world. No software team is exempt from dealing with the many threats that can infiltrate their corporate systems, development systems, operations, and even source code and the developers that you expect to honestly create it. Software teams should maintain a good level of security competence just like they need a good level of quality competence and operations competence. And just like these adjacent fields, it is never enough and we need specialists. Having a deep understanding of software development is a huge advantage, but security engineering really is a whole world unto itself. Thank goodness some people are willing to take it on.

Sales Engineer: Many enterprise and industrial products have such complex configurations, installations, and integrations that they require special technical assistance in the selling cycle which can't be handled by the Account Manager, and that is the job for a Sales Engineer. Sometimes a Sales Engineer must figure out a clever way to deploy the product or invent a workaround that enables a special situation to succeed. Other times they find the customer has a legitimate reason to need a feature, and the Sales Engineer will pass that information to the Product Manager for consideration and maybe commitment to deliver. Many Sales Engineers really enjoy seeing the diverse kinds of applications that customers bring, a bit of travel to customer sites, and the satisfaction of solving their problems and earning a win.

Support Engineer: What happens after a sale when the customer has a problem? Most enterprise and industrial product companies maintain a staff of Support Engineers for this purpose. This isn't simply a method of reducing the burden on the product engineering team because there is truly a different skill set for Support Engineers. They need to understand customer environments, other applications that may cooperate or interfere with the product, associated technical areas like system administration and networking, and especially how to debug tricky problems that may arise. While product development engineers tend to deeply learn a small slice of a product, it is the Sales Engineers and Support Engineers that really understand a product in all of its complexities and know how the whole thing works.

User Experience: There isn't a law of the universe that states coding engineers can't design great user experiences, there just aren't many good examples of it. Modern UI frameworks are a specialty unto themselves, as well as all of the best practices in user experience that have evolved since web interfaces and mobile apps were introduced. If you want consistency and an experience your users will enjoy and rate five stars, then you need a UX designer.

Database Architect: Databases with very large data sets can grind an application's performance, so it takes someone with a lot of experience in performance patterns and an analytical doggedness to design schemas and queries and routines that can scale and respond quickly, and to sniff out and fix slowdowns when they emerge. There are great technical differences between SQL and noSQL types of databases, and even between particular databases, so specialized technical expertise can run quite deep.

Data Engineer: There are some systems that produce copious amounts of data, and then some that produce way more than that. What does it all mean? Most software developers really don't know the tools and techniques needed to organize vast piles of data and process it efficiently to yield business value, whether it's internal metrics data or customer data. And there is a whole other layer of – who is allowed to see it? And are we maintaining compliance with the standards required of our business? How do we get data into and out of applications? Increasingly, we also ask – how can we inform machine learning to achieve superior results more quickly? Call the Data Engineer.

Project Manager: There are lots of variations of project management across many fields, some with their own professional associations and even certifications, but in this context we will narrow it all down to the field of Software Project Management. In short, a Project Manager's job is to make sure that the software gets shipped on time, coordinating any resources across the company that are needed to make that happen, and reporting on progress, blocking issues, and predictions. This field has been changing quite a bit in the years since Agile methodologies were introduced, and Project Managers have needed to become deeply involved in many of these software development processes.

Program Manager: Sometimes there is confusion within a company between the roles of Project Manager and Program Manager. Generally, think of a "project" as the delivery of code, and a "program" as being all of the additional non-code aspects that are needed for ongoing successful delivery and happy customers. (I know, oh the irony that we used to refer to a piece of software as a "program." But corporate-speak took over, just go with it.) This could include: negotiating trade-offs amongst other programs; planning budgets; communicating to customers; aligning with marketing, sales, and other corporate functions; managing vendor and partner relationships; and taking a large slice of accountability for successfully developing and delivering a product or service.

Product Manager: In short, the Product Manager defines what should be built, and the Engineering Manager directs the building of it. This is precisely because the Product Manager develops an intimate understanding of the market, competitors, customers, and internal finance and strategy positions that most of the engineers can't see. This is an awesome responsibility because it is the fulcrum around which the product can lean toward success or failure. Often, the Product Manager is given accountability for the growth and profitability of their products – essentially they are tasked with running the business for which the software is just a component.

Tech Writer: We often need to explain things to people having little or no knowledge about our product, but the explanations must be prose. To do this, a Tech Writer translates engineer-speak into English, usually for a technical audience but one that is not familiar with their product or domain. Not only must a Tech Writer be able to translate adeptly between these vastly different expressions, but they must like writing enough to do it for long stretches, and have enough of a technical background to avoid making errors.

IP Lawyer: The lawyers that help us to write and prosecute patents, and review our applications at the Patent Office, first are engineers. In a way an Intellectual Property Lawyer is a special case of a Tech Writer, but the language and style of a patent application is like no other form of expression, and takes a lot of training. IP Lawyers must know the whole patent process and how best to shepherd ideas through it, as well as many intricacies of patent law, handling contracts for confidentiality or licensing, advising executives and managers on IP matters, dealing with the judicial system when there are conflicts, and negotiating to reduce a conflict to a mutually agreeable conclusion.

Else, Exit

I would love to convince you about the wonderful career engineering can be, with every day being different and presenting new challenges, and the satisfaction of building things that have real impact on people's lives. But it's important to understand that there will be no coasting. In some professions, once you learn the needed skills, you can keep applying them and life goes on. But with engineering, and especially with software development, the problems get more complicated and demand that you confront ever more difficult challenges as your career progresses. Tools and techniques are constantly evolving and you must keep learning.

Some of us thrive in this environment, coping with continual change, and being comfortable with never being comfortable. But it's certainly not for everyone. If you are struggling, you may find one of the associated engineering fields listed above is better suited for you. And of course I've known people that figured out engineering isn't the right career path at all, with happy endings. So my advice is, appreciate that engineering just keeps getting harder and never seems to ease up; love it or leave it.

Reputation

LinkedIn has become the essential forum for professional communities worldwide. Your #1 job on LinkedIn is to be found. Imagine that you are safe and doing quite well in your job, not looking to make any changes in your life, but someone out there has an unbelievable opportunity where you would be a perfect fit and this would be transformational to your life. Would you want to hear from them, and at least be in the position to evaluate this opportunity? Well, that opportunity will never come your way if you are hiding.

If an opportunity is near to you, such as your former manager having moved to a different company and now is calling you to join them, then you got lucky and sometimes that does happen. But there are far more potential opportunities for you out in the world if only you can be connected to them and that connection usually happens through LinkedIn, which has become the industry rolodex for talent.

So how do you get found on LinkedIn? Your profile should always be current and complete; think of your profile as a replacement for your resume. It is a selling document and you are the product. Your title and summary should reflect the value that you have refined for yourself, and may hint at career aspirations. Build your connections to coworkers, present and past. As LinkedIn becomes more social, it is also weighing engagement. The more that you interact through comments and posting content, the more LinkedIn's algorithms will be impressed with you. These steps help to build your online reputation. If you don't have a reputation, you won't be found.

The world isn't completely virtual, so don't ignore the value of building your reputation within your organization, and to the broader industry outside of your organization. Grab any chance to meet with customers, or to attend industry conferences. Participate in open source coding projects. Attend local meet-ups and get out of your comfort zone and participate. Chat with other attendees, learn what they are up to, and make new LinkedIn connections.

Ethics

Somehow our world evolved into the condition where doctors and lawyers are licensed and bound to a professional code of ethics, but engineers are not, even though our creations can impact a vast number of people. If you have the interest, you can find examples of a code of ethics from several professional societies, but I would like to delve into two common cases that may cross your career path.

The first is dual-use technologies. Almost any technology can be used for purposes its creator never intended. Consider something as fundamental as an operating system, which can be used by the surgical gear that saves your life, or used by a weapons-carrying drone that threatens your life. Does the possibility of a negative use imply it was wrong for people to develop operating systems? The stakes were raised when the Web and Social Media were invented, and they are being raised again with accelerating improvements to Artificial Intelligence.

When Google won the US military's AI contract for Project Maven in 2017, there was a loud backlash from employees that didn't want their creations to be used for military purposes, especially given that many were hired under the credo "do no evil." This presents an important distinction since it isn't just a dual-use example, but a company's active involvement in military use. That's a personal decision whether you are comfortable working at a company serving military contracts, but a more straightforward decision for you to personally work on such programs or not.

Since I've worked in the US Defense industry, I can offer to you how I've made my own peace. Nothing we might ever do can stop the world from being inhabited by nasty, hateful, and violent people. Unfortunately no amount of wishing or negotiating can stop their violence except defensive use of violence, and I am extremely thankful to the people that serve their countries with the goal of restoring and preserving peace. To succeed at that mission, they need tools that are better than the bad guys.'

The second is job displacement. It is a normal by-product of information technology and automation that some people will lose their jobs because their skill was replaced by machines and computers. I have been a developer of such automation, and have even met some of the people whose jobs were being displaced because of my work. Again, you can make a personal decision to participate in engineering that directly displaces jobs or not.

Since the dawn of the industrial age, job displacement has been happening and yet the world economy keeps growing and employing more people. You may even be unaware that your own work is leading to job displacement. And yet society never seems to lament the loss of jobs once time has passed and we are looking at these technological disruptions in the rearview mirror. It's another example of the way that the world works, and in both dual-use technologies and job displacement engineers are central to the story.

Get Ready

Your job as a manager (present or future) with responsibility to deliver software may be titled in a number of ways, such as: Software Manager, Software Development Manager, Engineering Manager, Software Engineering Manager, or maybe something specific to the domain or function within your product or organization, such as Mobile App Manager or Cloud Infrastructure Manager. "Software" is used here in the very broadest sense, including data engineering, networking, operations, quality and support functions, and such.

The key elements to being a Software Manager, of any title, are: (1) accountability for the definition, development, delivery, or operation of software, and (2) managing a team of people to accomplish that. Let's confront our readiness to succeed at either of these responsibilities. Where can you learn to become a competent manager of software or other technologies?

A computer science or equivalent degree program might expose students to a minor level of project management, at most. Maybe you have experienced a team project where the work has to be coordinated among a few other students. Is that preparing you for managing a production software team? Not close. Even graduate and certificate programs in software management or technology management tend toward preparation for product management or technical aspects of project management – but not how to be a manager of teams and to master the development lifecycle. These programs named as "management" are really ironic.

The tradecraft of large-scale software development best practices does not have academic roots; it has been honed in industry over decades and diffused around the world through job migration, documentation, tools, books, videos, consultants, and conferences. And within that industry convergence still lies huge variations in practice.

Some business-oriented programs, such as an MBA, would expose students to elements of people management; however, this doesn't seem to have been a popular educational path for Software Managers. And even so, traditional perspectives on managing people spring from industrial activity or commercial bureaucracy. The normalized behaviors and processes to manage organizations of knowledge workers generally, and software developers specifically, is really quite recent and fundamentally different from traditional management practices. Every company invents some new aspects and the experiments are ongoing.

In any case, preparedness for a Software Manager role is on-the-job training, and the best training happens under mentorship. If you want to be a manager, look for a great manager and try to get on their team. Time to jump in.

Recap

The rest of this book will dive into the many aspects of building a career as a Software Manager, where success on starting that journey rests on a great foundation in engineering. I've shared some of my earliest engineering experiences because even as a rookie, or especially as a rookie, there are great lessons to be learned. Key among these are setting goals; taking initiative over your career choices; the importance of listening and helping others; and reacting to opportunities.

Design and development engineering and Engineering Management won't be to everyone's liking, so you can consider many adjacent roles. At the very least you should have some understanding of these roles because you will need to cooperate with many of these people. Even if you aren't a social media aficionado, professional careers are now inextricably tied to LinkedIn, so managing your online presence has become an essential part of managing your career. We discussed two ethical concerns that often arise in the course of engineering: dual-use technologies and job displacement through automation. Ultimately you can't get completely trained to be a Software Manager for the first day that you accept the promotion, but finding a mentor will be great preparation.

CHAPTER 3

Managing Engineers

Engineering is a team sport. We cannot build complex products and systems without first building teams. So when we talk about people management we are as much talking about team management, and managers have to pay close attention to every team member as well as the entire team dynamic. Doesn't that sound like coaching?

First Principles

Some professions, like law and pharmacy, have huge compendiums of knowledge to memorize and understand. Physicists also have a lot of knowledge of course, but much of it can be derived from a small set of first principles – why memorize a bunch of things when you can recreate them on the fly? I think of management in this way, that there is so much material to master, how would you know how to behave and react in every situation? Are there some first principles that we can apply to figure out how to succeed in new situations?

This book relates to all of that diversity and depth regarding management situations and how to excel at handling them. The task is made easier if you approach everything by holding on to a small set of first principles and learning to apply them consistently, so here is the list that I've discovered.

© David J. Asher 2024
D. J. Asher, *Mastering the Complex World of Software Management*,
https://doi.org/10.1007/979-8-8688-0841-8_3

Be respectful to others. We learned this in kindergarten and it still applies. Some situations can get frustrating and tense, and the best way to handle them is to ask ourselves how we would like to be treated. This guidance is not conflicting with a manager's need to delegate work, make tough decisions, or deliver bad news – just take a moment to reframe when interacting with others. And especially don't send an email when you're feeling bothered.

Stay calm and carry on. When executives or senior managers are lacking competence to understand and control an emerging problem, they tend to light a fire and then pull the alarm. It's not driven from a pyromaniac kind of delight, but a misunderstanding of how to get things done. Engineers discover, diagnose, and solve problems; they don't need to have a crisis to do this work quickly and effectively. Don't pull alarms, and try to bring calm when others do.

You are a fiduciary. An organization has entrusted you to get needed work done and to organize a team to do that work efficiently. In the way that software writ large has many interdependencies, a failure for your team to deliver expeditiously and with high quality will have many negative knock-on impacts. So always act like you own the place, knowing the whole thing could fail if not for the great integrity of your work.

Run a business. The software that you build is just a means toward achieving a business purpose. Ignoring that context is a recipe for building the wrong thing, or building in a way that works against the interests of the business purpose. The resources that have been granted to you are precious, so act like it's your money: spend wisely, and favor growth and profitability over cool tech or cleverness.

Be on time. Whether it's attending a meeting or delivering software against a commitment, being late is signaling that your personal time is more important than others'. That is a fast path to eroding mutual trust, and making it harder for others to be motivated to keep their commitments to you. If you can anticipate that you may be late for an unavoidable reason, give the other parties the earliest possible notification so they can plan their workaround.

Hire smarter people than you. The traditional view of managing people is the manager knows the work to be done and delegates pieces of the work to less informed workers. Software management is intellectually upside down; you should always be hiring people that are smarter than you are, at least in specialized skills. Respect that smartness and defer to their deeper understanding and experience at every opportunity.

Delegate decisions. Maybe you're thinking, "I'm a manager, I've made it! Now I can make the big decisions!" That's a fragile and unhealthy way to run a team. Even if you think a decision is yours to make, even if it looks easy, and especially if it looks hard, think again and challenge your team to learn how to make decisions in a deliberate way that considers all available evidence and takes as much time as is worth devoting to that decision.

Answer honestly. Not a single person reading this is dishonest, in that you never have the intent to deceive others. But let's say that you are asked to build specific software and you commit to a delivery date. If you don't have sufficient work estimates and resource assignments, you say to yourself that it's *possible* that you might deliver but know the likelihood is low. You're optimistic, but that's not the honesty that your customers and executives need.

Reduce entropy. Human systems are no different than any other complex system in the world, in that they tend to get messy (disordered, more chaotic) over time, seemingly just for being left alone. Degrading systems get less reliable and more costly to maintain, so they need proactive care and attention to reorganize them in clever ways to keep the encroaching entropy at bay. These issues pop up all around you, so keep your eyes open for it.

Drive innovation. Companies claim to be innovative and claim to want their employees to innovate, yet most are passive in their behavior, as if innovation will just happen. It doesn't, it needs nurturing and someone to drive it forward. Almost anyone can become an innovator or contributor, but they need to be presented with a worthy problem, challenged to solve it, and given the space and encouragement to do it. It's an active process, and you can lead it.

All the Hats

As if it weren't enough responsibility to direct the software development process while simultaneously managing a team for high performance, there is usually more required than wearing just these two hats. Depending on the day, the team, or a zillion other factors, you may be called on to wear any number of other hats. Or not exactly called on, as you might need to anticipate that you have to step into a particular role to effectively lead your team through an assignment or challenge.

Architect, quality engineer, bug sleuth, data engineer, Agile coach, project manager, SecOps, DevOps, CloudOps, vendor manager, strategist, cost analyst, process czar, customer support agent, party planner, facilities coordinator, immigration sponsor, tools admin, ... In addition to all of these hats, you must be an expert with a large body of domain knowledge specific to the product and industry you're working in.

If you're the kind of person that has to be the very best performer for every act that you do, let's settle now that you can't possibly achieve and sustain that level throughout your management career. No one can when confronted with such a wide diversity of skills and usually a tight deadline. Sometimes a task just needs to be disposed of, and your management behavior will be perfect if you can answer, "how can I get this done quickly, just good enough, with the smallest amount of work?"

There will always be too much stuff. Some of it you will delegate, some you will have to handle in the most efficient way possible, and some will get ignored until you-don't-know-when.

Someone can fault you for making a wrong priority decision and that's an evaluation that reasonable people should be able to discuss and learn from. But if you are not getting things done and cannot show your priorities, then it's hard to defend your performance. The same applies to spending too much effort on something that doesn't have sufficient value. Reasonable people can discuss how you considered options, but it's hard to defend missing a deadline because you were going too deeply in one activity at the expense of others.

Managers love to use a metaphor like "too many plates spinning" or "wearing too many hats." Overload will happen, and good management means finding a way forward in spite of the overload. Prioritize and compromise: these are the sharpest tools for surviving a manager's life of too much stuff and not enough time.

Change Happens

I once worked at a company that had a library – that's not unusual, but this library was floor to ceiling stuffed with books and a rolling ladder to get to them. Even if the room wasn't always filled with readers, its presence sent a clear cultural signal: part of your job is to learn. The software development environments that we construct, including all tools and languages and techniques, are only stable over short periods and have always been this way, so we need to keep learning, and need to keep changing. Every new job assignment presents unfamiliar domain knowledge that must be learned and mastered.

Sometimes we invest to learn something deeply only to find that it's gone stale and we're behind again. The body of knowledge of software development is a breathing, writhing beast. Technology marches forward and new best practices emerge and older ones decay, so to stay competitive your team has to stay current.

How do you even know what is current? You realize one day that you've been noticing references to an open-source program that the world seems to have grasped as if it's the industry-standard de facto shiniest tool and you wonder, *where did that come from?* This happens with databases, languages, security, frameworks, library components, and all manner of tooling. If you have a set of tools that work, why would you put effort into finding alternatives?

The first obvious answer is that you can't force change that often. Learning is expensive, grabbing a new tool or technique can be risky, and making a change to a production system could be very costly while the benefits may be suspect. It can be daunting just to perform even basic industry surveillance to understand what relevant technology trends are emerging.

At this moment some of you readers are working on a project that uses Java. Why do you think Java was selected? Door #1: Was it because the project founders made a careful consideration of all alternatives and arrived at a deliberate conclusion for the best language for this job? Door #2: Was it just familiar and the path of least resistance, or perhaps not even considered that there could be alternatives with improved benefits? Odds are on door #2.

This example points out that there are particular windows of opportunity for which there can be great advantage to survey the field of technology options and make a well-considered decision. The start of a project is one such moment, before committing a project to many years of an imperfectly fit solution. A second opportunity is when a tool is being deprecated or going through a major and incompatible version change, in which case you may even be forced to consider alternatives. A third opportunity is when you have observed that something in your environment is costing too much or causing too much trouble, in which case you need to ask if there's a better way forward than suffering. And a fourth opportunity is when a team member or someone outside the team presents a new option that is so compelling because it is pointing out a rising cost or trouble that you had accepted without complaint but now understand to be addressable.

Change Agent

You no doubt recognize there are costs to perform the analysis needed to understand when these windows of opportunity emerge, or the industry surveillance to find new solutions, so how much effort should your team invest? The right answer is greater than zero. But the more interesting question for your team is – how best to go about it?

You could make a specific assignment to a team member for them to explore something new, and complete the exploration by presenting a proposal to the team that shows key alternatives and the pros and cons for each. By rotating these assignments, you start building the team skill for software discovery and how to make rational decisions when selecting an option.

This is also a case where shared responsibility is helpful. If you establish a regular sharing session, say a lunch 'n' learn meeting once a month, you can get team members motivated to explore technologies that interest them and eager to share their findings. No pressure, no grading, just some fun and knowledge sharing.

From time to time, you will find a team member unexpectedly pop-up with something. It could be a very early and informal idea, and may not even have relevance to your mission, but it's always helpful to nurture a curious mind, so please take the opportunity to indulge them. But it could also be a serious endeavor that the team member didn't disclose earlier because they weren't confident in the outcome until they did some experimentation, as in "hey I just re-coded that Python service into golang and now it's blazing fast, would you like to see it?"

Of all the hats that you may need to don, you won't usually hear about "manager of change" as a critical role. Yet managing change is essential for any technology team to succeed in the long term and you, the manager, should play a leadership role in guiding your team to discover when change is important, and how to go about a sensible exploration and decision process.

Onboarding

When a new employee joins the company and lands in your team, they need to be onboarded. Larger companies may have an HR kind of orientation, but that is generic and has little to do with the business and technology that is your team's daily life and mission. More experienced workers have some foundation and need to understand the particulars about your processes, where documentation can be found, and who are the important contacts inside and outside of your team. College hires, interns, and workers with little experience are effectively starting from zero and need a lot of help.

Your project documentation is incomplete, partly outdated, disorganized, and scattered about. You have an org chart but that doesn't show what people are actually responsible for and who has expertise in particular areas. You maintain build, release, and other processes with critical undocumented elements and require priestly blessings. Your source code isn't structured in a way that anyone with a sense of logic would anticipate. I don't have to visit your office to know that all of these things are true. Then you take a new hire and drop them in the middle of this maze and expect them to find their way out.

Because of this situation, and because you can't quickly clean it all up just to impress a new hire, onboarding will work best when your team is prepared, and the best preparation is a written welcome guide. Think about all of these aspects of daily life in your team, and write up quick descriptions of source material, process overviews, collections of videos or other training guides, and list any pointers to dig deeper. It's a living document so ask the new hires to update and fix things as they wend their way through an onboarding journey with your team.

There are two kinds of relationships that are helpful to assign. The first is an onboarding buddy, who will be helpful to the new employee with all of the mundane but essential elements of getting work done. *How do I...?* The new employee will always have a first place to get quick answers without feeling like they are interrupting the team.

The second valuable relationship is assigning a mentor. The new employee's mentor will be helpful in understanding aspects of the project, details of assignments, reviewing work to give early feedback, introducing the new employee to various people, and help them with the social aspects of easing into a team that has already formed. Whether you are onboarding an industry veteran or a rookie, both an onboarding buddy and a mentor will be helpful relationships.

The one other thing you can do for a new teammate is to get them into an assignment as quickly as possible. All of the documentation and explanations in the world won't be effective without putting them into practice. I personally find it helpful to take a bug report as a first assignment because that forces you to look through the code, find your way around, ask basic questions, and put together the build process without concern for new code design issues or even having to understand terribly much about the whole project.

Shelter

What do your team members care about most? A short list would be (a) their boss isn't a jerk; (b) stimulating assignments; and (c) good reviews leading to increasing compensation and promotion. There are lots of other considerations, but these three are most often what make the difference between retention and departure.

I'm sure you're not a jerk and it is quite rare to encounter one. But it is possible that the bureaucracy and executives of your organization set some policies or issue directives that will make little sense to your team members, or seem to betray their best interests, or make their work life or home life harder without a visible benefit, or just tick them off with nothing more than a vague explanation. How does this reflect on you? And how do you keep a positive culture with your team and yet meet your obligations?

Good and caring people can seem like jerks when they implement nasty or nonsensical directives handed down from the bureaucracy. As we consider this kind of corporate mesh of weird policies, let's put aside the cases where the organization is asking you to do something that is clearly unethical or illegal, in which case you probably need to have a deep conversation with HR and yourself, but your answer should always be, "no."

There are some directives that you are going to dislike and they may feel wrong to you, yet are completely within an organization's prerogative to ask of you. One common case is selecting some of your team members for a layoff, or being told to create the grounds for a termination outside of a layoff, or the act of informing someone that they are being let go. You have to do it and won't like it, so what you can control is your own behavior and interactions with those people to minimize the burn that they feel – and they may feel like victims – and support them in their job transition as best as you can.

There are many less personal directives that you will encounter, and may object to, but don't have much choice about driving their implementation. These can range from HR policies to reorganizations to a specific technical mandate. The most straightforward presentation to your team members is to explain the directive and then open a question-and-answer session so the team members can work out their feelings or frustrations.

Be careful in positioning yourself, in that you want to be sympathetic to your team's concerns, but don't cross the line in saying "this is dumb but we gotta do it." You may be able to provide some insights and interpretations for your team that can be helpful, but in the process don't ever denigrate your executives or other parties in the organization. You may be managing a software team, but you are also a member of a management team.

I think about this aspect of team management as a kind of shelter, in that you are protecting your team to the best of your abilities even though the conditions in the environment may sometimes feel harsh and threatening. If you manage your behaviors and stay sympathetic to your team's concerns while fairly representing the organization's interests, the team should respect you. Also please appreciate that most organizations most of the time will have thoughtful and beneficial policies that are helpful or even joyful to everyone. Just not always.

Work Assignments

Work assignments are one of the most important aspects of a job affecting how an engineer might be intellectually stimulated, believe that they are making an important contribution, advance their career toward a promotion, and feel satisfied with their working life. Engineers can tolerate a great deal of frustration and even life disruption when they are working on an assignment that they love. How does your team get their individual work assignments? There are really two ways: you or a senior team leader makes an explicit assignment, or the team members pick the work items themselves. Let me suggest that your team practice both of these.

First let's consider work assignments from an efficiency standpoint. Most work assignments demand some set of technical skills, some specific domain knowledge, some familiarity with the existing code base, and maybe even relationships with particular team members or other

45

interdependent teams. So an optimal work assignment answers – who is the best fit for all of these criteria, and is available within the required time frame?

Usually you'll compromise a bit but someone on the team will stand out as the best fit, with "optimal" being evaluated as the shortest time frame for task completion. Most assignments are routine; they don't present a complicated decision and can be assigned fairly to any of several people, but the hard assignments should get deeper consideration.

Now let's step back and figure out if this is the really best assignment for your team and your project, over the longer term. What happens if you select someone that is missing a key skill, such as language familiarity? In this case, there wouldn't be much choice but to take longer than hoped for task completion while the assigned engineer first comes up to speed on the new language, or at least just enough to get the assignment done.

What if the assigned engineer wasn't familiar with the particular area of source code? They would have to take longer on task while they familiarize themselves with the existing code. What if they didn't know a key person external to the team and how the technical interface between their two teams' software operated? They would have to first spend time building a relationship and studying the interface.

This is almost always the trade-off in making assignments. Assigning a task to the resident expert on that task deepens that person's area of expertise and gets the job done quickly, whereas making an assignment to someone lacking in a particular experience results in a broader skills base across the team, likely a faster response to a future task, and better skills coverage when a primary expert is unavailable.

Looked at from this perspective of learning, it seems like making the assignment to a less experienced person is always in the long term interests of the team and will be the right answer. But of course, not so fast. There are times in the lifecycle of any project where time pressure is so high that you must make the most expedient tasks assignments, else you risk failing to complete a critical task on deadline. If your team is always under such time pressure that you can hardly make assignments to benefit long-term skills diversification, then that is a signal for having insufficient resources and maybe the team being overworked.

Self-service Assignments

What is a manager's motivation for encouraging self-service assignments? One reason is simply to offload the effort. Once a team becomes competent at managing their own task assignments, it's one less thing to manage. Another reason is because task assignment, like any skill, is learned from experience so it's helpful to get engineers involved. And in terms of the individuals, self-service assignments give them a level of agency over their working lives.

How could each team member make their own optimal assignments given all of the context that is required? If a team ran with 100% self-service assignments, it would probably find trouble with some tasks languishing while the most desirable get picked up first. There are usually some dependencies between tasks and it matters which ones get implemented earlier in the cycles. There may be high-risk tasks that people would rather avoid. Some team members might only pick the ones most comfortable for them, avoiding the learning part.

For these reasons, encouraging self-service task assignments is usually a benefit for a team, but really needs to have manager oversight, and in some cases the manager should make a few carefully targeted assignments, or overrule some of the self-service assignments to keep progress with longer-term team goals and fairness to all individuals.

The mechanics of self-service assignments and manager intervention can be made easier depending on your methodology. For example, if you are following Scrum and your stories are broken down to tasks that can be completed within a sprint and maintained on a backlog, then the question is whether team members can pull tasks from the backlog themselves or there needs to be a leader making those assignments. In any case the consequence of making an error is small because corrections can be made during the next sprint, therefore it is less risky to encourage self-assignments.

Ask, Don't Tell

One of the most impactful tools that you have as a manager is to ask questions, and by asking questions, I mean don't dole out answers.

Let's say that you know how to get a task done. You could simply assign it to a person and tell them how to go about doing it, and then you get success, right? But if instead you asked them how to get it done and they arrive at the same conclusion, they will own it and be more satisfied with the result. You may find that they arrive at a suboptimal or flawed approach, which then becomes an opportunity for a coaching moment and a deeper result. Or you may be surprised and delighted to find they have realized a better approach than you had thought of. In all cases, it's a bigger win to ask rather than tell.

Perhaps in bygone eras and other disciplines, a manager was expected to hold all knowledge about an industry and project, and then to make assignments, instructing their workers in detail. However most knowledge industries, and certainly software, turn the expertise relationship upside-down. The work is far too complex for one person to hold all material knowledge and skills in their head, so the manager has to accept the situation where their team members know more than they do and can solve problems without their manager's continual guidance (or interference). Yet you also can't foster a situation where you don't understand much of their work and they start heading off the rails, building the wrong thing, or writing lots of code that nobody asked for, or are just unproductive in their tasks.

So think of it as your primary job function to get your team members to think about problems in a way that yields the best results, and then to communicate back to you and others about the way they intend to solve these problems, and the quality of the work they have completed. These responses are best prompted with questions.

One-on-One Meetings

There is no shortcut for individual time with every member on your team. My personal rule is that everyone on my team gets a 1-on-1 meeting every week, pretty much no matter what. Sure, it's expensive on your time, and sometimes you may feel too exhausted to perform yet another 1-on-1 meeting, but I cannot stress too much how important this is for your team.

The way that I handle the logistics of a loaded schedule and a large set of 1-on-1 team member meetings is to front-load my weekly schedule with these meetings. I then set my work calendar with public read permissions so that anyone can see that I may have a 1-on-1 meeting and they are welcome to schedule a conflicting meeting, which I then prioritize and reschedule the 1-on-1 for a later time. Yep – constant juggling, but as a result I almost never let a week go by without everyone on the team getting personal attention.

In addition to every team member, you may have 1-on-1 meetings with people outside of your team: mentors, mentees, project leaders, peer managers, your supervising manager, and so on. These connections are really important to keep vibrant and nothing replaces a 1-on-1 meeting for building relationships and ensuring project alignment. It's often unworkable to fit all of them into a single week, so I will often schedule these outside 1-on-1 meetings at a slower rate of once every two or three weeks.

The content and duration of team member 1-on-1 meetings depends on the nature of your work, their seniority, and your relationship – it tends to get easier to delve into personal matters as you get to know each other and build trust over time. To start, you need to be able to get through an update of the current week's tasks. Since you already know what they're working on because of the daily scrum meeting, this meeting is a chance to dig deeper into particular topics: for your own better understanding, to validate that they are truly on track, and to coach them on approaches or changes that you can suggest.

If there is a change in work assignment for the upcoming week, it will be helpful to discuss that work to ensure they understand what is expected of them, emphasize the delivery target, counsel them on who they can turn to for help, and again to coach them. This meeting is an opportunity to provide immediate feedback on performance, especially to recognize outstanding results, heroic efforts, missteps, and misfortunes. If there are organizational or policy changes afoot, it is helpful to inform them as much as you can and ask about their feelings to give them space to express any apprehension or uncertainties. Do this even if there has been an all-hands meeting to raise the organizational topics.

After the task and org catch-ups, I suggest that you can rotate topics from week to week, such as their mentoring or mentee experiences, career goals, desires for particular work assignments, tracking progress on improving competencies, check in on their attitude about the team and their assignments, scuttlebutt regarding projects and company goings-on, ensuring they take vacation and other time-off, and a bit of social chit-chat to keep building familiarity and trust.

Performance Evaluations

The Human Resources department of any organization creates a process to evaluate the performance of each worker, which is used for assessing compensation, rewards, promotion, improvement, and occasionally becomes a factor in termination decisions. An annual review cycle seems to be the most common, but semi-annual and quarterly updates may also happen. If you've seen the performance evaluation process at one organization, don't think you've seen them all – the variation is enormous.

Let's separate several key aspects of the annual review: self-evaluation, peer evaluation, manager evaluation, improvements, rating, compensation, oversight, and career progression.

Expectations for self-evaluation can range from lightweight to intensive documentation. Most engineers and managers want to be documenting their achievements throughout the year so that it's easy to compile all of the evidence when it's time for the annual review. This is a good practice because it's easy to forget many of the details and especially the important contributions that you can be proud of. It is also helpful to document mistakes and mishaps, especially to share all of the lessons learned and how you reacted in these situations. Providing this information can also help a manager in their evaluation of team members.

Not all companies regularly practice peer reviews but it's getting more popular, and I highly encourage you to jump in and get your team into a good spirit because the results can be rewarding. Ideally, team members should receive anonymous comments from people within and outside of their team, and these should be complimentary reflections of their contributions and behaviors. When providing critical feedback, coach your team to avoid generalities and instead give specific suggestions for ways their peers can make even better contributions.

As a manager, annual reviews may feel like drudgery since there is a whole lot of paperwork to complete in a short amount of time, but always keep in mind that the results of your evaluation efforts have an enormous impact on each of your team members. Make sure that you are not filling out evaluations when you yourself are having a bad day, or let a most recent negative incident unfairly bias a whole year of good work.

Since annual reviews are enduring HR records and so impactful, I like to think of my evaluation comments in terms of long-term importance. For example, if there was a negative incident during the year, say, being late in a committed delivery, is it important to mention if you and the individual handled it completely, made a learning experience of it, and they showed improvement in follow-on work. Patterns of poor performance are important elements to document in an annual review, and then you can weigh the importance of one-off incidents because many of these are just the routine ups and downs of doing a hard job.

This approach should lead to a performance evaluation that celebrates achievements and fairly makes recommendations for improvements. Nit-picking small negative issues and being highly critical is generally not helpful to anyone. This is especially true considering that you have been doing your job well as a manager throughout the year, coaching team members, providing immediate and constructive feedback for any negative outcomes or behaviors, and especially being generous with gratitude and encouragement for work well done.

When suggesting improvements, take care to document actions that are feasible for a worker to succeed at while challenging them, but not so challenged that they are unlikely to succeed. Your suggestions should also be aligned with your team's needs and the worker's long-term career goals and short-term needs to be successful at projects that will help them get promoted. Don't give feedback that is overly generalized or abstract, because that is easy to dismiss and probably isn't actionable. If you want to convey a pattern of behavior as a generalization, be sure to include some examples.

Performance Ratings

Performance ratings vary in scheme from company to company, but are important as the quantitative basis of the bureaucratic mechanism to compare people and hand out goodies. Determining a performance rating is an easier task when you have a clear set of evidence demonstrating the performance level of each person on your team. The hardest part is assessing relative performance: does that mean you judge a person in comparison to others within your team? Perhaps one person on your team is a very rapid implementer but not so creative while another is highly innovative but painfully slow. Which one is "better"?

It gets tougher – how do you scale for different seniority levels and make an equivalence across a variety of job functions? And if it is considering people outside of your team so that the company can build a broad stack ranking, are other managers using the same standards for performance evaluation as you are applying? Hint: no, they are not. You can't reduce a performance rating down to a purely numeric exercise, so it's important to remove as many of your own biases as possible, and to fill information voids when you spot them. This process of creating performance ratings is always imperfect and may leave you feeling that you could have done better, but ultimately you should understand that it can't get done without some compromise and is nearly impossible to be as fair to everyone as you might like.

Once you have completed all performance reviews and ratings for your team, you're probably still not done. Many companies have a next-level oversight process where managers and directors gather and compare ratings across teams. This helps to normalize the review process as it gives managers a chance to discuss differences in their evaluation methodologies. It will also sniff out the outliers so that the management team can come to a common agreement about the most troubled performers and how to handle them, and also the most effective performers and how to reward them.

Sometimes an organization forces all ratings to be scaled on a curve and some people have to be the worst. If you have done your job well in hiring and training, there should be no worst people on your team, so you find it objectionable but must comply. The oversight review process also looks for individual ratings that may have had too much bias from a manager and sometimes you may find that one of your ratings is being overridden by a more senior manager. You won't like downgrading someone's performance and could try to appeal, but probably you won't have a choice.

If performance ratings are done well and are mostly fair, then compensation becomes more of a numerical exercise of scaling bonuses and raises according to ratings but keeping to an overall budget. It often feels like the biggest challenge in the performance evaluation and compensation process is communication with each team member. The company may announce something like an average raise or bonus, which makes people think of their own compensation relative to an average, but this is not at all the case. More highly compensated workers often get a lower percentage annual increase since their compensation basis is already higher. When you deliver someone's annual compensation change, you should acknowledge their important contributions, thank them, and simply explain their compensation level in terms of their performance review but not the details of the ratings mechanism.

Recognition and Reward

We do not all react in the same way to recognition. Some people crave it, while others can be highly self-conscious. Know your audience when attempting to recognize people that make a special effort. You can't go wrong with making private recognitions, except if you never do. Some organizations have well defined programs to recognize star performers in monetary and non-monetary ways. Peer recognition is also becoming more popular, where anyone can nominate anyone else for exemplary work.

A classical view of worker motivation proffers a contingent reward for achieving a goal – but consider this carefully before dangling a carrot. Doesn't your team already have a mission that they have internalized and that motivates them? When an engineering team has a clearly expressed and worthwhile mission, it's hard to hold them back from working extra hours to achieve or even surpass their goals. If that's the case, then what would dangling a carrot do? It can even backfire, treating people as if money were the key driver in their life and career, like they can be manipulated or coerced into over-performing. It is counterproductive when people take such pride in their work that they don't think of work as a monetary transaction.

Instead, consider handing out a reward after the fact. Not contingent, not promised, but unexpected. Now your worker's fine achievement is being acknowledged as gratitude. You can be appreciated as a manager who is being gracious rather than manipulative. A year-end compensation increase effectively works in this way; however, an unexpected reward immediately following a great achievement makes a clear statement about their value, and is an important element of building a deeper and more enduring relationship.

Career Advancement

Here are two true and contradictory statements: it is up to every individual to take responsibility for their own career, and it is up to every manager to help guide every one of their team members in their career advancement. The reason for the first is that so few managers pay any amount of attention to their team members' careers so no one should be under the illusion that someone is looking out for them. The reason for the second is that every manager should play a mentoring role helping to guide individuals, because that makes people more content in their job, more likely to be retained, and more likely to add value in the future. Don't be surprised if your supervising manager is unhelpful to your career, but that doesn't mean you should emulate that behavior toward your own team.

Career advancement can be understood in two parts: career goal, and promotion. Helping one of your team members to set their career goal can only happen through dialog, but don't expect one discussion to do the trick. You need to develop the trust of your team members that you are interested in their success, and have some perspective and ability to actually be helpful to them. That can take months and many conversations. It's okay for the results to be surprising and may not include your team in their personal plan. Your task in career coaching isn't necessarily to help your team members look to the next promotion nor to keep them in your team no matter what, but to help them understand their career options and plan their next steps toward realizing their goal. You may find it helpful to write down the results of career planning conversations so that you can track them over time and the team members can reflect on their explorations.

Most of the time, we expect that an engineer on your team will be looking for the promotion path to the next level of engineering as their career goal, in which case you can help them follow your company's Job Leveling Matrix for engineers. Your organization may already maintain a Job Leveling Matrix for most of its roles and particularly for software engineers, and if not I suggest that it's worth your effort to work with other managers and HR to create one that fits your needs.

A Job Leveling Matrix is a chart organized by job levels (i.e., pay grades) across the columns and various competencies are listed for each row. Reading across any row, you should see the skills and behaviors get more difficult and more abstract with each increase in level. Figure 3-1 shows an example of a simplified Job Leveling Matrix for individual contributor (i.e., non-manager) Software Engineers. Typically each competency would be defined in greater detail than is presented here and adapted for your special context.

Level / Competency	Engineer 1	Engineer 2	Senior Engineer	Principal Engineer	Distinguished Engineer
Experience	none	2 years	6 years	10 years	16 years
Education	B.S.	B.S.	B.S.	M.S.	M.S.
Coding Level	guided	contributor	independent	leader	expert
Design Level	function	module	feature	component	system
DevOps Level	guided	independent	improver	leader	leader
Supervisory	none	helper	mentor	coach	advisor
Communication	basic	documentation	presenter	advocate	evangelist

Figure 3-1. Simplified example of Job Leveling Matrix

The way to best use a Job Leveling Matrix with one of your team members is to focus on their current job level column and together form an assessment of their competencies. This should be as evidence-based as you can make it, giving examples of particular task and project successes that support your conclusions of competency. Don't look at this as finding and exposing weaknesses, but rather getting the person to understand what competencies are expected of them and how to go about filling in the gaps from their current performance.

Before considering if someone is ready for promotion, they should show solid achievements in all of the competencies for their current job level. You will have some paperwork to prepare a team member for promotion, and that will be made much easier when you have the evidence collected from your assessments of competency. But maybe the company further wants to see some promise of competency in the next job level before promoting, or perhaps some other factors. Make sure to clarify all promotion requirements with your supervising manager or HR business partner.

Misfits That Can Do Better

The great irony of software development is that it is an intensely social activity performed by intensely anti-social people.

Within this framework is a very wide range of personalities, talents, disorders, creativity, moods, cultures, language obstacles, disabilities, and communication challenges. As a manager you'll need to figure out how best to tolerate and integrate all team members and their sometimes quirky behaviors that could be resulting from this patch of humanity you've been given. But even so, not everyone succeeds in their role. Let's break this topic down into four levels in which a person could be misfit: underperforming, miscast, toxic, and egregious.

A worker's performance is measured relative to an expectation, therefore when evaluating someone as underperforming, the first question should be: is the expectation of their performance reasonable or not? It could be simply that their skill set or competency level was misunderstood, or that schedule pressure or other factors caused their expected performance to be set unreasonably high. In this case, don't punish them; explain the situation and commit to setting more appropriate expectations for future assignments.

Engineers will often be judged as underperforming when they are blocked by some technical challenge and have been unable to seek help and quickly get themselves unblocked. This problem could be viewed very narrowly as missing some skill or critical piece of information which is easily addressed. However the deeper problem is the person's comfort with reaching out for help, and with fully communicating their status. This would be a coaching moment.

Maybe it's about you and not them. It is hard to imagine but Thomas Edison had Nikola Tesla employed in his lab. Edison didn't know how to manage someone that was more inventive, and therefore more disruptive, than he was. So much of technology history could have been different had Edison figured out how to work with Tesla, nurture him, and exploit his startling inventions. But on the other hand, Edison also had every right to expect all of his employees to work within certain boundaries. The mixture just couldn't work.

Misfits That Need Your Help

Another common cause of underperformance is a temporary emotional struggle such as having a bad day, struggling to cope with stress, lack of sleep, or external factors such as family problems that are interfering and preventing a worker from realizing their fullest potential. This is also a coaching moment; however, you need to be careful and sensitive about personal discussions and especially health issues, trying to get just enough information from a person for you to understand the nature of their underperformance.

Life will challenge all of us from time to time, so it is important for you to ascertain if the person's problem can be addressed, and for them to appreciate that this issue is in fact negatively impacting their performance and must be addressed for them to succeed in their role. Each of these underperformance episodes can be handled as short-term and a normal part of managing that may not require HR involvement.

If there is an underlying personal issue such as a mental health challenge or substance abuse, these are well beyond a manager's ability to be helpful, so HR involvement is probably advised. If an episode turns into a pattern of persistent underperformance, then certainly you would be well advised to get HR involved because it would soon start reflecting on your own performance and putting a drag on your team.

The typical HR intervention may be to connect the employee with professional resources that can help with their problems, which may already be part of their benefits. With or without such services, you and HR may come to the conclusion that the employee is not performing because they aren't a good fit, and commence with a Performance

Improvement Plan. This is a detailed document describing the worker's performance issues, and a set of milestones that they must achieve to prove their restored competence. The consequence of succeeding at these milestones is to maintain their role, under a presumption that the issue has been resolved. If the worker fails to achieve the set milestones, the result would be termination. In this way, a Performance Improvement Plan transparently recognizes a performance problem and gives a fair opportunity for the worker to set themselves right, else manage their departure.

Misfits That Must Leave

A different cause of persistent underperformance is having been miscast into a role where the worker is unlikely to ever be successful. A person could be perfectly healthy and unbothered in any way, perhaps even being very smart and a self-motivated hard worker, and yet still not achieving their potential. You may suspect that this person has been misjudged in some way, and that their skill set and competencies really are not matched for their role. A good person in the wrong role is not likely to succeed.

Strictly speaking from an HR perspective, a miscast person is underperforming and therefore their manager should write a Performance Improvement Plan that sets conditions for correcting their underperformance. However, you already know this won't work when the employee has been miscast. I suggest that, since a manager has a responsibility for their team members' career guidance, the first course of action for a miscast worker is to have an open conversation with them about their career goals and competencies, and help them find a more appropriate role either within the company or outside.

A toxic worker may be underperforming or may be satisfying technical expectations; however, they exhibit behaviors that are causing stress and underperformance among their teammates. This is not a sustainable situation. HR may require a Performance Improvement Plan which could take months to work through, in which time the toxic worker may be causing continued stress and damage. You will need to work with your supervising manager to handle the situation, possibly reassigning the worker until the PIP has been completed and termination can happen. In any case, for a toxic worker, termination should be your goal.

Egregious behaviors would include harassment of other workers, blatant violation of company policies, and wrongful acts such as abusing the expense reimbursement system or violation of the Foreign Corrupt Practices Act. Your action is to call HR and make a full report. These are the few, and thankfully rare, cases where termination can happen quickly.

Recap

Every management assignment is unique so there is no playbook that will give you the right answer for each situation, but developing a set of first principles can prepare you to take the right actions. My list is: be respectful to others; stay calm and carry on; you are a fiduciary; run a business; be on time; hire smarter people than you; delegate decisions; answer honestly; reduce entropy; and drive innovation.

When you manage engineers, you will be wearing a lot of hats and working in a dynamic environment that seems to be changing continuously – after all, software development is a creative process. As a manager you will need to encourage change in your engineers and help them navigate the many changes in technology, industry, and your organization. You also need to foster a productive environment through an onboarding process and sheltering them from distractions. Work assignments are a key factor in job satisfaction for your engineers. It matters how tasks are assigned to individuals and they will evolve faster as more responsibility is delegated to them. Engineers will also perform better if challenged with probing questions rather than if they are handed a solution.

Performance and evaluation are your responsibility for every individual on your team, and you will find it helpful to use frequent 1-on-1 meetings to build their trust over time and really get to understand their performance blockers. Sometimes a person doesn't perform well and you, their manager, need to understand the cause so that you can take the best corrective action which could range from helping them through mentoring and training, to moving them to a better fit role, and in the most severe cases removing them from your organization.

CHAPTER 4

Leading Teams

Sometimes, you will be assigned a team that is up and running where you may be replacing a manager. But if you are starting from zero, or only have a partial team that needs expansion or staff replacements, then team building will be a top priority. This chapter will then look down, look up, and look all round at the many aspects of managing a team or department within a larger organization.

Hiring Process

You may need to grow your team, and the first thing that you need to settle is the goal of your hiring process. What kind of talent are you seeking and how will new people affect the team? Broadly speaking, there are two fundamental approaches which I'll call *filtering for competency* and *selection for talent*.

In filtering for competency, an organization is defining and controlling the hiring process in a precise way to ensure that no one gets hired that doesn't at least measure up to a nominal level of job competency. This is particularly true for the top tier of technology companies because, if you can imagine hiring continuously to support an enormous organization, you would need some way to prevent the hiring process from degrading with informalities, shortcuts, mistakes, favoritism, or bias. If an organization needs to tightly control the hiring process to ensure quality,

© David J. Asher 2024
D. J. Asher, *Mastering the Complex World of Software Management*, https://doi.org/10.1007/979-8-8688-0841-8_4

you may not be able to deviate much when building your own team, but you can have confidence that the results will at least lead to competent employees.

You don't need to be operating at gargantuan scale in order to filter for competency if that is your stated goal, it just takes a bit of up-front planning. Consider that your hiring process should incorporate some testing and specific interview questions that are designed to gauge technical competency, and then you can see that it isn't practical to design many variations for highly differentiated skills. Therefore this approach tends to hire generally competent people without being highly selective for particular skills. It can be favorable for candidates as it opens opportunities to fill a job that requires skills they may not have, as long as they pass the more general competency filter.

In selection for talent, consider your current team and its goals, formulate the skills that are missing or insufficient, and then target those skills for hiring. With each new hire, ask the question, is the candidate bringing something new to the team, with complementary skills or perspectives that will make the team broader and more capable? This kind of hiring takes more effort as each position is crafted to add unique value, then the interview process needs to validate these qualities with each candidate. In some cases, a candidate's potential benefit gets exposed during the interviews, and may even impact the hiring process such as writing a new tailored job description or selecting a different team for placement.

A secondary benefit of selecting for talent is building diversity in your team. Think of "diversity" in its broadest sense – experience diversity, intelligence diversity, cultural diversity, and diversity of perspective. In addition to adding skills with each new hire, if you widen your filter and prioritize selecting for talent, you will build more diverse and stronger teams as a result. The most vibrant form of selection for talent is playing Moneyball. The reference is from the 2003 book by Michael Lewis that describes how general manager Billy Beane built a winning team by searching and selecting for very specialized talent to fill particular roles.

The hiring process gets kicked off with a written job description and completion of a job requisition and approvals, presuming that you already had budget allocation for the new positions. Your organization probably has some templates for job descriptions that you can copy and modify, but it's worth putting some care into writing JDs to attract the best candidates. Don't fill the job description with a lot of boilerplate – get to the point, make sure to highlight the special skills that you are looking for, and emphasize your mission. You want the potential candidates to be able to quickly scan the job description and envision themselves in that role.

Sourcing Candidates

Some studies have shown that upwards of 80% of hiring depends on a personal connection. Whatever the real figure might be, personal connections are a critical part of managing your own career, and helping to build your team. Potential candidates can be sourced in a few ways: from your team's personal connections, posting the open position on an online job board, searching for candidates, networking at industry events, and recruiters. Most of these methods have become dominated by LinkedIn, so you need to get familiar with it as a recruiting tool. Don't be timid about getting out to industry meet-ups and other events, as they can be great for networking and building connections. Get your team members involved, too.

I implore you to avoid or ignore the automated resume screening tool which is probably already a part of your HR department Applicant Tracking System. Maybe this is helpful in evaluating low-level commodity skills across very large quantities of people, but is in no way a best practice for the highly evolved and specific skills needed for advanced professionals in technology development. There is no shortcut for human review of candidate resumes if you want to find talent.

It's worth noting the impact that a remote working policy has on the hiring process. If your organization and team will allow remote working, your candidate pool has geographically opened wide – at least to anyone within a much larger commuting radius, likely to anyone within a time zone or two, and depending on your practices, to the whole world. This can generate a huge volume of potential candidates, as compared to only searching within a limited geography near your office when all staff are in the office full-time.

LinkedIn has made it exceptionally easy for candidates to submit applications to open positions, generating a lot of unqualified candidate noise in the set of leads. The most effective way to manage overload in a screening process is to put a few short essay questions in your online application, which will filter out anyone that isn't serious about your opportunity. With a smaller set, you can use your eyes for screening, or if you're lucky enough, the eyes of a trusted inside talent sourcer or recruiter can help.

Interviews, Tests, and Presentations

Few companies train employees for interviewing, and it isn't a natural skill for most engineers to pick up. The best advice for any interviewer is to be prepared: have your questions ready prior to the interview, and review each candidate's background through their resume and LinkedIn profile. Check to see if you have some common connections. To get more junior engineers accustomed to interviewing, have them shadow a few real interviews so they can more deeply understand the process and range of candidate response styles.

When kicking off a hiring cycle, the hiring manager (let's presume that it's you) should select several interviewers and give the hiring panel guidance on the position. They should have the job description, additional commentary about the position, and some assignments for each person to specialize their interview in some way that minimizes overlapping topics.

Some companies like to perform general intelligence testing as part of the hiring cycle, which can range from formalized IQ-type tests to brain-teaser questions from certain interviewers. I'm highly skeptical of their efficacy – oh, these tests can identify people that can pass these tests, but is that actually correlated with more productive and innovative employees? There just isn't evidence to support that. There are many aspects to intelligence, and these tests set a narrow filter that would tend to normalize the organization in a particular way, which isn't how you build strong teams having diverse capabilities and perspectives.

My preference for testing smartness is to examine a candidate's work in depth, and the examples are posted right on their resume. Pick one or two projects, and drill down. Keep asking questions to elicit greater levels of detail, and finding out how much they understand about that particular technology, about the designs and solutions that address key problems, and what exactly their personal contributions were. Whatever level of smartness this candidate may have, a superficial performer can't fake their way through.

Coding tests are an interesting case that has become very popular for coding professionals at nearly every level, and there are now online tools that help in the evaluation process. Coding tests can be calibrated for generalized computer science skills, or get quite specific on the competency level and precise skills required for your job. Some candidates have become well trained in taking these tests. The following is why I believe some level of code testing is a critical element of a hiring process for software engineering talent.

There is a sliver of humanity that can think in code: they are given a problem description and can then build the coded expression that solves the problem. While a great many people are trained in computer science ranging from coding camps to graduate degrees, only a fraction of those are adept at the craft of coding, especially when it comes to solving unfamiliar problems and designing complex systems of components. It is the function of a coding test to separate job candidates into those that can code and those that can't, and you don't hire those that can't. The test doesn't need to be complex or tricky; even simple coding programs can discriminate between coders and the rest of humanity.

I have encountered enough candidates presenting themselves as accomplished coders with great resumes and even passing traditional interviews but that have demonstrated little competency in writing code, that it's clear some kind of test is required to prove basic coding skill. In a few interview situations I recommend eliminating the coding test: for managers, for PhD-level candidates, and for candidates that bring open-source coding samples such as their GitHub account and can clearly explain their own contributions.

It's not unusual to ask manager candidates to make a group presentation of some sort, but on one team I also used it for almost every technical candidate, even college hires. The format is to gather the hiring panel for the presentation at the start of an interview cycle, and start with the candidate introducing themselves and briefly sharing their background story. The candidate then presents some project that they worked on and explains their contributions, using whatever format they are comfortable with, typically slides or whiteboard, and then complete the session with open questions from the panel. This sets an information baseline for everyone on the panel, saving time in the subsequent interview sessions. It also demonstrates the candidate's communication skills, and basic ability to interact with other engineers. Why go through all of this? A coding job is so much more than coding.

Candidate Evaluation and Decision

In cases where you have more job openings than you can quickly fill, you may be interviewing a single candidate for one or more positions, and the decision needs to determine whether the candidate is right for the team, allowing some flexibility on the assignment. In cases where there are multiple candidates competing for a single position, your decision becomes one of selecting the best fit candidate for the role.

It is helpful to have a candidate evaluation framework defined, preferably at the start of the hiring cycle. This would enumerate the important technical skills and soft skills that are expected of the candidate, and allows each interviewer to organize their evaluations and compare notes. Some of you with a quantitative bent may be thinking that you can apply weights to various criteria, grade the candidate on each, and out pops a hiring decision if they numerically pass a threshold. I don't agree.

Think of a hiring decision in this way. If anyone on an interview panel votes against hiring a candidate and feels strongly about it, do you really want to bring the candidate onto the team? If not, then we are really advocating for a unanimous decision. Is that feasible? It becomes practical if the person moderating the interview panel, which could be the hiring manager but not necessarily, takes the approach of driving the panel to consensus in a post-interview evaluation session.

After the interviews are complete and the hiring panel meets to deliberate, the first round of interrogation for everyone on the panel is checking for *red flags*, warning signs that the candidate is clearly not a match for the team for some particular reason. This could be a technical deficiency such as a glaring rookie mistake on a coding test, a personality quirk like showing frustration at an interview question, or cultural mismatch like exhibiting a towering ego that would misfit against your largely humble organization. If a candidate tells you that they have been successful and don't need the money, stay away; their motivations are not aligned with your organization. The evaluation session could be a quick negative result if a red flag surfaces, especially if it is noticed by more than one interviewer.

The second round is a brief report from each interviewer about their findings, essentially making their own argument for a hiring recommendation or not. The panelists should challenge one another on the findings, in particular to more deeply examine strong positive and strong negative observations. Going through this cycle, the panelists tend to convince each other of the rightness or wrongness in hiring this candidate. Make sure that everyone on the panel has a chance to contribute.

The hard part of an evaluation panel is when you are mostly resolved but a few sticking points or uncertainties remain. The panel moderator should then attempt to close on these last few points and drive to the consensus decision. If the panel concludes positively but with someone raising a strong objection, then it should be clear to everyone exactly what the objection is and what risk is being taken in making an offer.

Finally, a panel may conclude that the candidate is worthy to be hired by the organization but just isn't a good fit for the job they were interviewing for. The right thing to do is to find another team that is likely to be a good fit and make a recommendation for hire. That second team should then be able to make a hiring decision with an abbreviated interview cycle.

Budgets and Spending

There are generally two large classes of expenses that an Engineering Manager needs to budget and track spending on: headcount and operations. All of the other things that are generally shared across the organization and not particular to your team, like personal computers and travel expenses and productivity software and office space, are usually allocated to other departments or aggregated at a higher level.

Headcount (often called "resources") is usually measured on a per-person basis rather than in currency, because it's just easier to budget and make assignments in this way. Usually personnel budgets don't allocate for people by their individual salary, because this can change throughout the fiscal year, is highly variable between individuals, and would just add a ton of complexity with little benefit. Instead, headcount is pretty much literally counting heads irrespective of their salary level. Your organization may define a Full-Time Equivalent (FTE) engineering salary metric for the purposes of converting from employee headcount to currency in the budget. If you need to plan for hiring three people into your team in the coming fiscal year, and you can defend the need to do that, then the budget adjustment is simply adding 3 to the headcount.

Contractors may be handled in the same way as employees and lumped together with employee headcount, or handled as a separate headcount budget item. Alternatively, contractors may be handled as a separate expense amount for the known contract value, which becomes a kind of operations expense apart from headcount.

What is the right level of headcount spending for engineering? This is one of the hardest business problems in software development, because there is no formula that gives you the answer. Some types of organizations, such as non-profits, IT departments, and government agencies, will view software development as a pure cost center and spending will always be constrained relative to needs. For-profit companies that understand the way in which software investment can drive future profits are more likely to fully staff engineering teams.

Typically, engineering budgets tend to swell when a company is cash-rich from high profits or investments, and tend to constrain when faced with an uncertain economic outlook or lowering profitability. Tech companies sometimes go into an irrational exuberance pattern of headcount inflation when profits are soaring or investors are throwing cash at you.

What do you do when your leaders increase your headcount budget beyond your request? You will need to come up with plans that lead to market-valuable feature improvements or new products, and get cracking on hiring. What do you do when your leaders chop your headcount budget? You will need to make some hard decisions about your staff, terminating contracts, and possibly letting valuable people go, while changing your plans to wring the most benefit from the remaining staff.

Operations expenses are what you spend to build your delivered software or run it in real time, pretty much anything but people. When building software that is shipped to a customer, the operations costs are usually low, maybe including some computing resources and licensed software. But if your team is hosting online services on behalf of customers, the underlying cost from an infrastructure service provider and other service partners could be significant and ongoing. It's also becoming more common for software development infrastructure and tools to be hosted in the Cloud, in which case those are non-trivial ongoing operations costs.

Scale and Structure

Your team has a structure, whether explicit or implicit. An explicit structure will have managers with sub-teams, or team leads that are directing sub-teams, where each sub-team encompasses a group of engineers that are either working with similar skills or working on a common project. When the structure is implicit, there hasn't been a need to formalize, but there are usually still groupings that may shift from time to time that help make teamwork more efficient and break down complexity into feasible tasks. But there is still a structure.

Who gets to report to you, and who should report in to a manager within your team? That usually depends on the size of your team, and which people would most greatly benefit from having direct reporting to you. Once you have a team structure that is large enough to include managers, you generally want to delegate as much as possible to them, balancing that there may be some functions, such as architecture or project management, where you want a more direct line of sight to what's going on and more continuous influence.

All structures break when pushed to scale, and this is as true for software as it is for organizations, so you can expect to make structural changes as a team grows. There are usually signs of stress when an organizational structure is experiencing growth, such as some people not understanding their role, or people getting burned out from overwork. *Reorg* isn't a bad word; it is the expected result of success.

Is there a way to figure out the right structure for a software team? There is. Conway's Law roughly states that the software we build looks like the team that built it. This result is inescapable because of the way it reveals human nature and communication patterns. Start a project with architecture: decompose the problem by defining the major components that minimize communication between the components, and then take this architecture and assign team structure accordingly to the components. That's Conway's Law in action.

It may be hard to get a perfect mapping from an architecture onto a team, but getting close leaves you in a position that's more likely to succeed. The reason is simple: once you put a sub-team together and give them an assignment, they will coalesce to build a component or some functionality that is self-consistent and bounded. Conversely, if building a component requires the cooperation of four people assigned across four different teams, don't expect a pretty result. When people have a specific and detailed shared purpose, put them together.

Team and Staff Meetings

As a manager, you can schedule two kinds of standing meetings in addition to any software development process meetings: all-hands team meetings and leadership staff meetings. In an all-hands team meeting, you want to be as inclusive as possible with every individual contributor invited and expected to attend. In a leadership staff meeting, you want to convene the smaller set of team leaders that influence the work of others, whether they are Engineering Managers, Project Managers, tech leads, architects, etc.

If you are managing a team of individual contributors, an all-hands meeting will be smaller and can be less formal. If you are directing several managers or other directors each having teams, the meeting is much larger and quite expensive in terms of productive time lost to the meeting, so these are typically scheduled less frequently. All-hands meetings need an agenda with relevant topics else people will vote with their feet.

An all-hands meeting is an excellent opportunity to broaden the perspective of your engineers by inviting presentations from product managers, marketing managers, finance, sales – anything that can add context to the work they are performing and enabling them to understand the value that their work brings to the company, to customers, and to the market. It can also be an opportunity for your supervising manager to get more familiar with individual contributors and their work, because they are usually far removed from it. If an individual has completed a great achievement or innovation, have them get up and explain it. If there is a significant process change needed, have the tech lead get up and explain it.

A staff meeting, if you are managing individual contributors, is a smaller and more informal affair. A staff meeting for a director would typically include all direct reports, some of which are probably Engineering Managers, while some may serve other roles such as architects or project management.

I recommend that you don't spend time in staff meetings with round-robin status reporting that can otherwise be handled with memos and is probably just a redux of the stand-ups and other meetings anyway. While you may believe that there is a benefit for everyone on staff to hear what everyone else is doing, individual behavior is usually to check out when others are reporting their status and wake up when called upon. So do staff meetings have value?

As a general rule, be considerate of the time that people are taking out of their workday to attend a staff meeting, so formulate a meeting agenda with meaningful topics. Get your staff in the habit of contributing agenda topics to you in advance of the meeting. Gathering your leadership is a critical time where you can all focus on a few urgent problems, align your priorities and goals, resolve resource imbalances, discuss personnel challenges, plan for mid-term and long-term tasks, argue about technical direction, and generally enforce that your leadership itself needs to work as a team.

If you announce something at a team meeting, you're not done. If something is important, repeat it. Say it in team meetings as well as 1-on-1 meetings, document it, reinforce it in conversations. People are naturally suspicious and resistant to change, and need time to get comfortable with a change and embrace it. How do people know if you are serious about something if you only say it once? Maybe people have questions or reservations or need to challenge this important thing, or maybe some people interpret it differently, so you need to provide multiple opportunities to get feedback and to let people speak what's on their mind. Ideas that bring change need repetition to sink in.

In the Hierarchy

Whatever level that you are managing within an organization, there is context, and that is almost always within a management hierarchy. Like it or not, intended or not, all large organizations become a bureaucracy. There will be the people you are managing, peer leaders within your department, various agents in other departments, the more senior manager that you report to, and executives. The series of managers each reporting to a higher-level manager right up to the CEO is often called your "chain of command." Most organizations produce org charts, typically a set of diagrams drawn as boxes representing people as individual contributors or as the leader of a team, with lines representing reporting relationships. It sort of looks like a pyramid with the most senior manager on top.

You are never just managing your team, you are also managing up and sideways, at all times. Managing up is advocating for the interests of your team so they can grow and get the best work assignments, and advocating for yourself as part of your own career advancement. Managing sideways is a matter of balanced cooperation and competition with your peer managers, both within your department and across to other departments.

The structure of management hierarchy has been so successful and enduring because it can scale to almost any size that is needed to be organized, and is efficient at dividing work so that complex projects and operations can be accomplished. The increasing power and compensation that comes with managing at higher levels also sets up incentives for ambitious people to work for greater achievements in their careers. Those are the good parts. Now let's look at the awkward parts.

Once promoted into a higher level position, a manager will be assigned responsibility for a broader portfolio which may include some functions, products, services, technologies, and even disciplines that they have little or no experience with. This aspect can be isolating for a manager since it places them in an authoritative position but usually without adequate training and lacking a support system for decision-making and leadership, yet needing to present themselves as fully competent. We are all put into a position of being an imposter.

This should be no problem at all since, as engineers, we can figure things out! In the eighth grade we were the smartest kid in the class and have never gotten over that! Yeah, engineers tend to have a confidence bias, especially over soft people-oriented skills and business problems because we've had no difficulty in mastering the "harder" technical skills. Except, that just isn't how the world works. These are very difficult disciplines to master, yet the management hierarchy demands actions and decisions in far too short a time to first do enough learning to get good at it.

All of this means that we accept a lot of management mistakes because of guesses and assumptions over topics that we're too proud to admit we just don't have the competency for, or maybe don't even recognize our own weaknesses. The easiest way to circumvent making these mistakes in our authority is to avoid taking risks, evading new and unfamiliar initiatives, deflecting decisions to others, and trying to find someone else to blame when failures happen. This spiral to risk aversion is a built-in feature of management hierarchies. It reinforces the dynamic that a large organization should keep doing the same thing and that deviation has a high cost. It takes an enormous sustained effort to reconfigure an organization to behave outside of a risk-aversion mode and into higher performance.

Information Rising

The other reason that middle and upper management roles can be isolating is the way information flows from lower levels in the hierarchy. As a manager, it is an essential part of your job to report up. What does that mean? It means that you need to consolidate a lot of diverse information and compress all manner of technical details into a meaningful summary of your team's progress, accomplishments, and challenges. From an information perspective, that's how a hierarchy works – every level must digest information in order for it to be consumed at higher levels which can then be used to make increasingly strategic decisions.

Here's the rub: your reports are spin. Your reports are selective, subjective, optimistic, and downplay or disguise any negative events and trends.

Let's say that you are just phenomenal at doing your job as an Engineering Manager. You discover that there is a problem in your team that might cause a delay in your commitments for delivery. Do you report this problem? Maybe not because, as you figure it, these are technical details that are hard to explain; similar problems happen all the time and we have been able to solve those, so there is no need to cause alarm and report it. Maybe that's a fine decision, but maybe the problem does result in a delay and then it turns out that you knew all along and never reported on it, so that doesn't look good on you. With the best of intentions and your perfectly competent performance, you still may be filtering out the very information that your supervisor needs.

Now let's assume that you are quite a lousy manager (which I know you absolutely are not, but this aspect of bureaucracy is critical to understand) and have somehow survived unmolested in your role. Probably you survived by misreporting to your supervisor. Are you being dishonest? Well, perhaps you are just applying your spin, because it's your judgment that determines what to report. How would your supervisor know that your bias is potentially hurting them, especially if you are quite good at spin? It may be difficult for a senior manager to discern the nuanced difference between less competent judgment and deception.

There are two compensating behaviors to address this information gap, both for you and your supervisor. Your reporting needs to be a learning process between you and your supervisor, converging over time to the exact level and style of reporting that they most need. Providing too much information overloads your supervisor and may even obfuscate the important points, and providing too little, or avoiding the more painful topics, may cause harm. In general, start the process by reporting too much and take feedback from your supervisor, but especially make sure to highlight the most important issues as headlines. Follow this golden rule in reporting and you'll do fine: *never surprise your boss.*

The compensating behavior for your supervisor, and for everyone managing in the hierarchy, is to perform skip-level meetings. This would be a 1-1 meeting, or maybe a small group meeting, between your supervisor and your direct reports, without you being present. An organization that demands this behavior of its managers will be far more efficient at aligning perspectives, catching problems, and identifying weak managers. An organization that does not enforce or encourage this practice is exposed to failures caused by critical information being blocked and ultimately hidden from executives.

You are now starting to count the hours that would be spent in skip-level meetings and you are realizing that it's just impossible to fit this activity into your busy schedule. However, you can learn from the best. President Lincoln would hold visiting hours from ordinary citizens twice every week. Quite literally, anyone could walk in and talk with the President. As he described it: "... though the tax on my time is heavy–that no hours of my day are better employed than those which thus bring me again within the direct contact and atmosphere of the average of our whole people. Men moving only in an official circle are apt to become merely official–not to say arbitrary–in their ideas..."

Information Sinking

Information flows in two directions, of course, but not with any kind of symmetry. As a manager, you will receive information from your supervisor and their peers that is related to your work, such as assignments, corrections, customer feedback, changes in product strategy, changes in budgets, and so forth. Now you have information filtering decisions to make. How much of this should you inform your team, and how to present it?

If you present your team with all of the information that you receive from the hierarchy, you will distract and overwhelm them. Sometimes you receive information that is tentative, just a heads-up. If you pass this along to your team and it doesn't come to pass, then you've needlessly ruffled them. Sometimes you receive information that is privileged and cannot be passed, at least not in any detailed way. And sometimes you're just privy to hearsay because of your position but can't validate it.

The tougher judgment calls happen when you intentionally decide to withhold information from your team. You can think about the information filter to your team in this way: what is the absolute minimum information that needs to be passed to them in order for the team to remain effective at their jobs? Any additional information carries risk that you could misinform or unsettle them in some way. As a manager you have a job to do that is shielding your team from corporate BS, and at times it can seem like a struggle.

There is a whole other kind of downhill information that flows from your HR department. Some of it will be ordinary, such as policy changes and deadlines for annual performance reviews, which you will mostly just share and help to explain. Larger organizations have increasingly more policies that need dissemination and training sessions that are required, which you have to support and encourage your team to support.

From time to time an organization may engage in training that is none of these things, which usually indicates some kind of executive initiative. These may stray from the business essentials that you support to attempts at cultural influence that make you wonder. Some of these may truly be useful and targeted at addressing real concerns about employee performance and culture. Others may be material that consultants sold to your executives who didn't fully understand the depth and consequences of rolling out this training and how it may not really align with the organization's values, but it's good business for the consultants.

Suck It Up

As a manager, you will be handed directives from time to time. Most of these are just fine; you've got engineering work to do and everything lines up nicely. You just may need broader context or guidance, or help resolving between choices where you don't have sufficient control to make a decision on your own. Sometimes, not so much.

You may be handed a directive that you don't like, for example implementing a special feature for one customer where you can't see the wider market benefit, but maybe there was a very influential account manager advocating strongly for their customer, and no one asked your opinion. In the best case, it's a mild dislike so just suck it up and keep on engineering. You can ask questions, but you should understand that your supervisor isn't interested in hearing a complaint every time you are handed a directive.

Some directives are harder to accept because of their impact. Perhaps you were requesting to expand your product in some innovative way, or were requesting extra staff to make improvements, and these were denied. The denial probably isn't about you, but rather about resource and strategy trade-off decisions that are made at higher levels. This is the normal work of managing a complex technology business. Again, suck it up, don't complain too much, and get on with your engineering.

It should be less common, but you may receive a directive that deeply bothers you. For example, you may be told to make use of a vendor whose service you believe to be low quality, or to put most of your resources into a feature or product that you believe won't result in an outcome that is successful to your business. These may be cases where it is reasonable for you to challenge the directive, maybe even it's your responsibility to challenge the directive, but also understand that there may be influences at play that you can't see and ultimately you should realize that you can only complain so much. Management hierarchies don't like a rebel in the ranks.

Of course, staff reduction directives are some of the hardest to deal with because they directly affect careers and lives. In a formal layoff situation, your job as a manager is to implement the reduction plan. There may be some room for negotiating on behalf of particular individuals that you can defend as a poor decision to terminate their employment, but on the whole a staff reduction that has been decided at executive and HR level cannot be avoided.

There is one situation where you do not suck it up, and that is when you are given an unethical or illegal directive. A clear case of this (in the United States, but may apply elsewhere) is a violation of the Foreign Corrupt Practices Act that is very explicit about permissible interactions with foreign actors. Most companies take the FCPA very seriously to the letter of the law, but it's certainly possible that the incentives of closing a large deal could cause a company to try and bend some rules or cover up an irregularity. Call HR.

Politics

All of the managers in a bureaucracy are people, so one outcome is unavoidable: politics.

For an imaginary moment, let's remove any nefarious motivations and negative connotations, and presume that you are part of an organization of well-meaning, well-trained, and competent managers. You and the peer managers within your department are cooperating to build complex systems or maintain ungainly operations, but you are also competing for scarce resources, higher impact assignments, compensation rewards, and promotions. Even in the best of circumstances, there can't be cooperation without competition. Budgets and rewards are capped, so it becomes a zero-sum game. Some of you will naturally be better at playing this game than others, so do you get resentful at the more successful ones? And what's the impact on the organization, and on you, of that resentment? This is the unavoidable core of organizational politics.

Now let's lift the restriction that all players are well-meaning, to which there can be many shades of gray, ranging from oblivious to diabolical. Since I've witnessed these actors often enough even within organizations that are proud of their high hiring standards and healthy culture, I am confident that it's prevalent. On the oblivious side, a manager could be completely non-malicious but so singularly focused on their own success path that they are not considering the impacts and possible collateral damage from their actions. We would usually refer to this person as "not a team player."

Toward the diabolical side would run intentional bad-mouthing and back-stabbing, smearing someone else's reputation to put themselves into a better position. Such people could be abusing their positional authority, or contaminating the social network that exists within every organization. Sometimes they may actually believe that they are operating in the best interests of the organization, but spouting uninformed opinions can be very damaging, and it is hard for other people in the hierarchy to discriminate between subject matter experts and self-professed authorities wielding ulterior motives. Such damage is devilishly hard to repair.

These are all normal circumstances and the whole crux of politics – and why less competent people can win – because there isn't necessarily a good response to other people that are behaving politically in a way that doesn't seem to align with the ideals of your organization. The best defense for yourself is to build as many healthy relationships as you can, and maintain a positive reputation through your great achievements and help to others. The best defense for an organization is to identify negative political actors and be intolerant to behaviors that don't comport with the definition of a healthy culture that the organization's leadership is working so hard to build.

All politics isn't bad. You may find a mentoring relationship with a senior leader that is helpful in your work and career advancement. Call it favoritism, but a meritocracy should shine a spotlight on its top performers.

Leadership Development

Run this thought experiment. Your organization has ambitious goals with many competent people in place; however, you are constrained in hiring such that you may acquire rising talent straight from college and that's it; no senior leadership can be hired, and no outsider with industry experience can fill an open role. How could you succeed in such a situation?

Let's look at an open role in your team, knowing that you have the responsibility to fill this role in order to achieve your goals. The reason why your first impulse was to hire from the outside was because you looked at your team members and didn't see the right skills in any of them. A next step might be to look broadly across the whole organization for a person having the needed skills, and then transfer that person to you if you can. If you still can't find the right skills match, then you are out of options – you will need to settle for the best fit, the person having the smallest skills gap relative to this open role.

Now what do you do with this person that is missing critical skills? Again you are out of options and will need to train them. Training can take many forms, such as a mentor that can guide them, or more formal internal or public training, or giving them the time and space for self-education. Do you believe that such a person would fail, that they couldn't learn these new skills in a reasonable time? If so, that attitude would fly in the face of the presumption that you've already hired people that are smart and fast learners. Maybe training this person will be a slower process than if you could hire from the outside; however, the upside is that you have taken someone that is already familiar with your work environment and raised their value.

This is the decision that you implicitly make every time that you hire someone from the outside to fill a role: denying an employee the opportunity to expand their skills and advance their career. But let's say that your organization actually works in this way, then how best to go about identifying employees to take these new roles? You would probably want to be intentional about it, trying to identify the most promising candidates to take new roles, and providing them with training to expand their skills so that they are ready to take on challenges beyond their present skills. This is Leadership Development.

To be fair, let's also make the exact opposite argument. If your organization only recruits talent from college graduates and 100% of open roles are filled by employees, then you are effectively operating in a bubble.

Information and even culture gets bounced around in an echo chamber, and doesn't get scrutinized by a newcomer that looks at your behavior from an outside perspective and realizes that you are doing things in outdated or inefficient ways. Even more critical, in such a fast-paced industry as software development where new tools and techniques are constantly evolving, getting current on best practices demands that different kinds of talent sometimes enters the organization and mixes it up.

Okay, we can see there are advantages to a Leadership Development approach and advantages to acquiring outside talent at practically every level. The problem with most companies, and especially fast-moving tech companies, is a lack of balance where Leadership Development is practically non-existent. We can do better.

Recap

A thoughtful hiring process is the start of building a great team, and we discussed two different approaches to sourcing candidates, interviewing, and making hiring decisions: filtering for competency and selection for talent. Your approach should align with the goals you have set for the team that you want to build. The structure of your interviews, including code challenges and other testing, will have a great impact on your ability to make decisions as well as the candidate's perception of the opportunity.

The next biggest influence on your team is the budget that you must work within, which for software development teams is usually based on headcount rather than money. Many teams will also have an operational side of their budget. Scaling a team will present challenges, and you should expect to make reporting changes and sub-team structures as your team grows. A good part of team building happens within team meetings, which you can encourage if you lead your team into meaningful discussions rather than simple round-robin status reporting.

In most organizations, your team exists within a context of other teams and a management hierarchy. As a manager you will act as an information filter in the ascending direction by reporting your team's status, challenges, and accomplishments, and in the descending direction by selecting certain information to share, emphasize, or hide. You may be tasked with executing some top-down commands that you do not like, but you have accepted a responsibility to carry them out in a professional manner.

Since a management hierarchy is made of people, there will be politics. You don't need to become political in order to thrive, but you do need to be aware of the political context and learn how to navigate yourself and your team within a bureaucracy. One of the key indicators of your success as a manager is your ability to develop leadership within your team, including your own succession.

CHAPTER 5

Vibrant Culture

We all want to work in an environment where our efforts and skills are appreciated, where we can work productively with little frustration, where we feel safe in doing our work and interacting with others, where we have a shared sense of purpose, and where we have confidence that our organization's leaders are behaving responsibly and guiding our growth. This kind of culture doesn't happen by accident. You and your cohort of managers must exert deliberate effort, else the results may be a descent into an unpleasant and disorganized and unproductive mess. It takes work to build and keep a vibrant culture.

Abstractions and Rituals

It should be intuitive that a rule or policy (or even a law) can't possibly consider all situations that it is intended to administrate, so we tend to describe cultural policies in terms of abstractions of the conditions we want. *Always be nice!* The problem is, abstractions aren't actionable. They are easy to dismiss because applying them to a situation requires recognition and judgment. Going from an abstraction to real-world practice is not a thinking path that most of us easily perform in the moment of a situation. Abstractions may express the general outcome that you want, but they don't clearly express the actions and behaviors that people need to get there.

© David J. Asher 2024

D. J. Asher, *Mastering the Complex World of Software Management,*
https://doi.org/10.1007/979-8-8688-0841-8_5

A culture forms in an organization no matter what, so many leaders wisely set about getting ahead of the process and making a serious attempt to define a culture they believe to be healthy and advantageous, and they usually start with abstractions. These abstractions are compiled into a list, not too short and not too long. Then the list appears on meeting room posters, in employment collateral, in career promotion requirements, and gets airtime in executive speeches.

So what is the connection between these abstractions and culture? Do they achieve their intended result, or do executives just presume that since they defined their intended culture, it must be working as planned? Given that people can't reliably take action on abstractions, we should not have confidence that we are building the intended culture. There needs to be something to bridge this gap and these are rituals, meaning a defined behavior, whether defined positively or negatively, that people can perform repeatedly with little thought. Let's work through a few examples.

Let's say that you define a ritual: "Prefer to send short communications over chat/text, prefer to save long form or persistent information to wiki, and prefer not to pass project information as email and attachments." The abstraction is really "Be open with information," but people are so accustomed to using email they may not realize the way that it is a private communication between select parties and therefore hides information from other team members. So the ritual is explicit in its behaviors – what to do and what not to do in particular situations, and over the long run people will figure out that teams perform better when they are sharing information openly and that they should stop using tools that work against that benefit.

Another ritual might be: "Never break an API (Application Programming Interface)." Many developers believe that they control an interface since they define it and maintain it, but that isn't true. The consumers of the API have made a significant investment with their business depending on perpetual compatibility and they will be deeply disrupted if the API is ever broken, hence the developer really doesn't have control. Developers may believe that they are creating a welcome benefit for their customers by making an improvement, but when that results in a broken API, the cost often far outweighs any benefits and the developer should have considered an approach to improvement that just doesn't cause a break. The relevant abstraction might be "Respect your customers," since breaking an API shows a lack of concern for their situation and is therefore disrespectful, but here again it is unlikely that a developer might interpret this abstraction in terms of API management.

Let's try one more ritual: "Do not drink at your desk." This sounds strange, but I worked at a company that strictly adhered to this policy. There were legends about how it started, but its impact was irrefutable – people had to drink so they would gather at the cafeteria. A cafeteria culture then emerged where people would regularly plan meetings in this public place and frequently meet serendipitously, helping to broaden social networks and cooperation, and overriding our feeling that a social drink in the middle of the workday is wasting time. A relevant abstraction may have been "Be social and build community" but the tendency to drink unthinkingly while you work and be content with desk-bound isolation would have overpowered any urge to get up and be sociable, so a clearly defined ritual was needed.

After repetition of rituals, abstractions emerge and culture forms with people behaving in consistent ways. In other words, building a vibrant culture is a bottom-up exercise in selecting preferred behaviors that ultimately achieve desired outcomes, not a top-down exercise in slogans and posters.

Management by Rituals

Having made the pitch that rituals are a more effective mechanism than abstractions for building culture, let's look more deeply into how they are used, because if you take a careful examination of your organization you should find dozens if not hundreds of defined rituals.

"Ritual" has a religious connotation: we do things because we are told to do them and are told that those are the right things to do. Told with absolute certainty; no thinking is required and no challenging of the rituals will be tolerated. We believe: our organization is growing and successful, therefore we must have the right rituals since they lead us to success, right?

Except that there is always some other successful organization with different and even contradictory rituals. We never seem to ask whether our rituals are causal factors in our success, nor attempt to prove whether those assumptions hold true. We don't even wonder.

You just need to accept and implement the rituals that someone before you, someone that maybe even left the organization, just made up. Literally, thought they had a great idea, just made it up, and issued their decree. Maybe your company even has a guiding principle that says you need to accept and implement these rituals even if you disagree.

We may be performing rituals that are counterproductive or not aligned with our own best interests, or maybe even downright damaging. How can we identify those, and prove the cause and effect? That's where a scientific mindset and a bit of curiosity is helpful.

Let's take a common example of hiring. Most organizations have a process for hiring, some quite detailed in the nature of screening and interviews and such, and may also be prescriptive in the manner of getting to a hiring decision. Let's open our curiosity and ask a few questions. Are we actually getting the talent base that we believe is the intention of our hiring practices? Are we turning away some of the talented people that we are seeking? Could we be faster or use less effort and get the same results? What is the impact on candidates – and our reputation – from our hiring process?

If you have a hiring process and can't answer these questions based on the historical evidence of actual hiring, then your process is running "open-loop." If some hiring rituals are working against your best interests and causing divergent results, how would you even know? Now apply this reasoning to any and all of the rituals that you are asked to perform, and in all likelihood you can see that your organization is not getting actionable feedback in terms of its rituals and culture. Do you have any feedback mechanism in place to catch and correct detrimental or harmful rituals? Do you even try? Do you even wonder?

Engineering is the craft of applying known practices to solve familiar problems over and over, and doesn't seem to have much appetite for scientific inquiry. If you start thinking about any ritual as a hypothesis rather than a commandment, you may be able to make improvements that actually result in the culture that you're trying to build.

Essential Meetings and Not

Here are some common complaints: (1) we have too many wasteful meetings; (2) I don't know what's going on; and (3) can we serve more food at meetings? It's okay to feel conflicted about things and sometimes you will get this kind of ambiguous feedback. So let's break it down.

Those of you involved in Agile methodologies for software development are familiar with a set of meetings – a daily scrum, weekly backlog grooming, sprint planning, retrospective, etc. These have converged over time to attempt to be the smallest set necessary to keep a software team aligned and productive, with meeting rituals that reduce wasted time. Whatever your team's workload and methodologies, it's always worth spending a bit of effort, once in a while, to consider improving your meeting formats. The more a team is involved in this process, the less they are able to complain about these meetings. Okay they may still complain, but they will also realize that they have some agency.

Here's a funny thing about human nature and meetings. Whenever I've told engineers that they can leave a meeting when the content becomes less relevant to them, they won't. I've often stated, right in a meeting, we're about to shift to the next topic, and those of you that aren't interested may leave. They won't. So they complain about wasted time and then when you tell them to stop wasting time they won't. Whatever.

If your team is fairly isolated with few dependencies, then there may not be many more mandatory meetings for them to attend. But the more interconnected a team is with other teams or other organizational functions, their meeting load goes up. This is the nature of building complex systems where more communication is required to keep things on track. Engineers may dream about being able to spend 100% of their time focused on isolated development, but large scale software can't work that way. It's also much more healthy for themselves, for the team, and for a project, when people have regular interactions so that they build familiarity and can then solve problems much more quickly.

Not only is there a tension between having meetings and productivity, there is also an information sharing element within meetings that addresses the feeling people have about not knowing what's going on. When you get this comment from someone, challenge them – what is it that you feel uninformed about? Did you incidentally hear about something that you thought you should have already known? If you can distill the situation into a specific kind of information, you may be able to include that as part of your meetings and help the spread of good information.

Having food at a meeting can build a more social atmosphere. If you are forced because of time constraints to hold a meeting during lunchtime (which you should never, ever, do, but let's say that you really have to) then it would be considerate to provide lunch. Sometimes a snack in a morning or afternoon meeting can also lighten the mood. However, I find food at a meeting to be a distraction. My preference is to hold social meetings where food and drink are provided, and hold business meetings with no food, not usually mixing these two very different kinds of meetings. You do you.

Damned Surveys

Well then you're wondering, how do people on your team really feel about rituals, culture, meetings, and so much more? Oh it's easy to get that answer – send out a survey! Please, not so fast.

Organizations frequently use surveys to gain understanding so that they can make improvements to policies and culture; however, surveys are often poorly constructed, in part because effective surveys are devilishly hard to design and we aren't trained to create them, in part because most of us don't understand statistics and will draw erroneous conclusions from highly biased samples, and in part because our motivations may not be true.

How do you feel when you receive a survey? I guess you feel the way I do: *Oh, no, not another survey!!* Or, you feel tricked because the introduction states it will take just two minutes of your time and you find that it's really long. You try to answer a few questions, but the multiple-choice responses don't cover the answers that you'd like to give. What does that 1-to-10 scale mean and how can I tell the difference between 6 and 7? The wording of a question is confusing or can be interpreted in multiple ways. The survey omits the question that you really want to answer. Perhaps the survey topic makes sense but instead it is asking all kinds of questions that don't seem to be relevant. The survey seems safe to answer because it's anonymous, except it is asking qualifying questions that can pierce the veil of anonymity without much trouble. Or maybe you're just burned out from getting far too many surveys.

There are so many ways to create a survey that will frustrate its participants. Do you think that the last survey you created, or the next one, will generate fair and actionable results? Why would you think that – did you try to compensate for all of the design factors that result in a lousy survey, and did you have it edited before release, or test it with a few trial participants?

The most fundamental deceit of surveys is that they generate a set of data, so we conclude that we have found truth because we see data, even when that data is so biased as to be lying to us.

A simple example to illustrate. A bunch of people leave a team and the company wants to know why, so they send out a survey, getting 50% participation. Right off the bat you can see that the survey has a survivor bias, since the most important people – those that have already left – could not respond. Then the company interprets a 50% return rate to be pretty good, except the half that didn't answer are the very people that are already so cynical and considering leaving that they wouldn't respond, so the 50% of returns has a terrible selection bias. The survey gives multiple choice responses for the question "What frustrates you the most?" with one of the choices being "your manager" and nobody selects that choice, even though it is the right choice, because they don't believe they will be treated fairly after the survey. How come the survey isn't anonymous? And anyway, the last four surveys that were sent out had no visible consequences or even discussion, so why would anyone bother with yet another useless paper exercise?

When we are presented with a survey, we assume that the presenter is interested in learning something about us that they don't understand, and they want to gather evidence to make fact-based decisions. But really, surveys are often designed, or unintentionally biased, to confirm a desired outcome, not to learn. In the very presentation of a question, the survey can lead the participant to an answer that does not yield discovery but biased confirmation.

Nearly every survey that I've seen is plagued by these kinds of distortions and dysfunctions. And none of the above even gets to the most basic flaw in the concept of surveys, which is that some people may simply feel uncomfortable, indignant, threatened, untrusted, or in any other emotional state that would fail to get an honest response or any response at all. Surveys can be useful, but it takes a lot of work to achieve credible and actionable results. Otherwise they may do more harm than good.

Measuring Sentiment

Well after that beating on surveys, what can we do? If we are intending to foster a particular culture, then it's critical to measure sentiments within the population in some way in order to confirm our assumptions, and make corrections when in error. Some of you might be yelling "focus groups!" but I'm not going there because focus groups are even harder to design, administer, and interpret than surveys.

The problem of measuring organization or team sentiment is not so different from the general marketing problem of understanding a customer base or potential customers, so let's try from that perspective. Surveys for marketing purposes often suffer from the same deficiencies described above; however, some can be effective if there is a marketing analytics team that applies experience and scientific principles to the survey design, careful selection of participants to reduce bias and noise, and statistically justifiable interpretation of results. So if you insist on conducting surveys against your organization, hand it over to the professionals.

Another powerful marketing measurement technique is the in-depth interview (IDI) process. The power of a survey done well is that it can reach a large sample of the population, given the assumption that an unbiased selection within the population will be reliably representative of the whole. The limitation of this approach, even with a well-designed and valid survey, is that it can't go deep to explore what some of those participants might really be thinking, nor discover truths that would be impossible for a survey to reveal if they hadn't been anticipated and designed into the survey in the first place.

An IDI allows for depth and surprise by designing a structured conversation with open-ended questions, and inviting a small group of respondents to engage. Taking extra care to select the participants is critical because the sample size will be small. Even if the IDI administrator is unknown to the participant, the fact of a person-to-person discussion raises the stakes and sets up a more likely honest and complete response.

Typically responses will be transcribed, and having a structured set of questions enables the responses from multiple participants to be aggregated in some data-meaningful way. For sure, there is a good deal of work to read through all of the IDI responses and derive a set of conclusions. The point of an IDI is that knowing just a few individuals deeply can be more enlightening than knowing (or pretending to know) a larger group superficially.

Real-Time Surveys

Given all of the above, I would like to share with you a very specific survey approach that I have practiced with teams to great effect, often achieving over 90% participation and yielding highly meaningful and actionable results. At the start of an all-hands departmental meeting which would be held every four to six weeks, I would ask everyone to pull out their phones and click on the survey link that I just sent out to them, and take a few minutes to fill in their responses.

The survey is simple and anonymous. Every time the survey starts with the same three questions: How do you feel about the company? How do you feel about your team? How do you feel about yourself and your work? The responses are on a numeric scale of 1 (lousy) to 5 (fantastic). Then there is one open-ended question that is topical for the moment, and one completely open-ended question for anything the person wants to express. That's it, always five questions.

Toward the end of the meeting, I pull up the metrics and charts from the survey and project them so we can review the results together. Then as a group we scan through the open-ended responses and pick a few for immediate discussion. Within a few days, the leadership team gathers to review all of the responses and selects a few to take specific actions, with the critical follow-up of reporting back to the team at the next meeting.

There tends to be many comments because nearly everyone leaves a comment – this part is truly amazing and not what I first expected, but consider what is going on with the sociology of this kind of survey. Since time is given to everyone at the start of the meeting, there is no excuse to avoid participation, and in fact there is some latent peer pressure to participate. Then the very public group evaluation demonstrates that everyone else is contributing to the betterment of the team, has some deep insights and is showing their sincerity, and that the team leadership is not just listening but actively participating in the process. This leaves almost no room for cynicism or unwillingness to fester in the team.

One last point – the numeric scale for the first three questions enables real data collection and analysis. Because these questions are consistent and sampled on a periodic basis, you can show trends over time. Aberrations tend to jump out. The numerical trends won't reveal underlying causes, but they will indicate when a problem exists and alert team leadership to pay attention. For example, after one survey we had a single data point for someone feeling lousy about themselves. I talked with one of the Software Managers about the importance of tuning in to each person to see if someone is struggling, and he said, "Oh no, that was me, I was having a really frustrating day!" So much to unpack there.

Authority and Influence

It is a key feature of any hierarchical organization that authority is vested with certain individuals as "managers," such that they are held responsible for getting work done and are accountable for the results – this is a functional authority. They are also responsible for the performance and improvement of people that report to them – this is a resource authority. Engineering organizations tend to vest both of these authorities into the same person, the Engineering Manager, but that is not always the case, and not always in a complete sense.

For example, the authority to deliver a project may rest with a Program Manager, and the authority of what product to build may rest with a Product Manager, either of which may report to the Engineering Manager but often the reporting is done another way. Some organizations define a "matrix structure" where people effectively have two managers for functional and resource authority, which can make the organization manager-heavy. The positional authority of an Engineering Manager to direct resources for the completion of projects or fulfillment of services is presumed and rarely made explicit, but seems to always be recognized.

When one of these managers with positional authority wants to exert influence, they can usually just direct people to that end, or in the worst case must negotiate with other managers that have the required positional authority, and it is expected that they do so. Why do managers try to exert influence? It's usually in furtherance of their goals, which will get them rewards if completed to satisfaction.

However, engineering is a complicated endeavor. The people that best know how to build and deliver a project, or that understand critical factors that were missed by others, or that have key insights into product requirements, or are thinking about inventions that can dramatically alter the path of success – they may not be recognized as having positional authority, perhaps having no expressed authority at all.

"Influence without authority" is the characteristic of an engineer that succeeds in influencing an organization to do the right thing even though they are not in a position of authority. Imagine that an engineer, holding some critical perspective, cannot make their views known to the people in authority, and cannot be convincing when attempting to influence direction. This clearly becomes a situation that puts the team and organization at greater risk, so a culture that enables influencers has a greater chance of achieving success.

But influence without authority also applies to managers: after all, management fundamentally is getting people to do things, and that sometimes means influencing people that do not report to you. When your success depends on the work of people outside of your positional authority, your own success may still depend on their actions and results, so you must influence them. Even when people do report within your positional authority, their commitment is far stronger, and your trust relationship far deeper, when you have influenced them to do the right thing instead of commanding them.

Deference to Authority

Engineering teams have been trending toward greater diversity, with much of that diversity resulting from building teams that increasingly comprise people from different regions around the world. Each country, and many regions within countries, has developed its own peculiar set of social characteristics. Even though we are all individuals with unique talents, being raised in a particular region imparts some traits that derive from the place we were raised. In general it's not helpful to get too deep into these effects on people and certainly not to stereotype any individual; however, there is one powerful trait we inherit from our home society that is useful to understand when managing people and teams: deference.

In this cultural sense, deference means the extent that a person defers their own perspective to another person in positional authority. For example, I was raised in the metropolitan New York area that is known for its very low deference culture, probably because of its unique history of Dutch tolerance, free-wheeling capitalism, and nearly unimpeded immigration and diversity. Challenging authority and confronting people directly isn't seen as disrespectful; if anything, it shows greater respect to engage someone – anyone – in pursuit of a better outcome.

For a high deference culture, questioning authority would be seen as disrespectful, even taboo, to the extent where it hardly ever happens. In some contexts, such as a military organization, high deference might be essential, but for engineering work high deference can prevent a team from making critical improvements and discoveries, precisely because the person in authority can't possibly know it all and make all good judgments. Just because low deference may be a beneficial behavior for engineering, doesn't mean that it's easy for people that were raised in a high deference culture.

If you are a manager and come from a high deference background, you will need to examine the interactions with your team and make sure that people are comfortable challenging you when it's appropriate, even if that is uncomfortable for you. Conversely, if you come from a low deference background, you need to appreciate that some team members won't be comfortable questioning people in authority and you will need to find ways to break down that barrier else you won't be getting the feedback and guidance that you need to succeed.

Open Information

This seems intuitive: organizations will function more productively and make fewer mistakes when information is readily available to anyone that could make use of it. "Readily available" doesn't mean that an information holder is willing to disclose their information when asked, because that presumes the requester knew about such information in the first place, and further places a burden on the speed of communication. Therefore an open information culture would make documentation and communication available to teams continuously and without filtering, with as wide a distribution as is permissible. Yet we usually are not intentional about setting policies and selecting tools based on this principle.

First consider our default form of internal communication. Email seems like an efficient way to communicate in many situations; however, its information hiding powers are extraordinary. For many common uses email is excellent, especially if the communication is more formal or of a broadcast nature, such as HR sending out a policy update. The problem with email is that it is a private communication between sender and recipients, so it inherently hides its content from the people that aren't party to it. An attachment travels from the sender and gets stored on the recipient's computer, never being shared in this process.

Consider all of the essential and routine communications within a team, and between teams, in the normal course of software development. When it was common for a software team to be collocated in an office, engineers and their managers would frequently communicate person-to-person and use email as a supplement. If there were impacts of information hiding from the use of email, they were minor and usually offset by meeting and talking. As teams became distributed and eventually became partially or fully virtual, interpersonal communication was the first victim, so if email became a key method of communication for a team, a lot of information was hidden from the team's members and its manager.

A similar information hiding problem happens with documentation stored on individual computers or even network drives – you have to know exactly where to look and hold the required permission to access a document, and even then you couldn't tell if you were looking at the most recent version.

If you want to build an open information culture, you can't base it on exclusionary tools.

The open information properties you would want for effective team communications support text chat discussions arranged by topics and defaulting to open permissions (e.g., text tools like Slack or Teams). The open information properties for effective documentation would support topic organization and browsing, search, and versioning (e.g., wiki tools like Confluence, collaboration tools like Basecamp or Quip, and document tools like OneDrive and Google Drive). Similar open information principles should apply to your source code versioning system, and even group calendar and meeting schedules if you can make that happen. When you build your organization on open information tools, an open information culture develops around that.

Recap

Most organizations define top-down abstractions that they intend will foster a culture of productivity and happiness; however, abstractions aren't actionable and so often fail to achieve the intended result. Instead, rituals can be designed to build a particular culture from the ground up and will work precisely because they are actionable; however, their impacts may be narrower. Beware of rituals that are arbitrarily designed by someone thinking they had a great idea but didn't really think through all the consequences. All-hands meetings will be an important part of building and maintaining a vibrant culture. Some people will complain that they are forced to attend too many meetings, and at the same time complain they don't get the information they want and need, so make sure that you are generous with your information sharing at all-hands meetings.

The way to ensure that a vibrant culture develops is to regularly measure the sentiment of your teams and individuals. Online surveys can be used but are very difficult to design and end up providing management with misleading data sets. Two alternative approaches for sentiment measurement are in-depth interviews and real-time surveys.

As a manager, you are anointed with positional authority. Given that you have built a team of really smart independent thinkers, wielding your authority with too much command will not build trust, but using your ability to influence is far more powerful. Also finding the natural influencers and working closely with them, regardless of their position, will help to align the organization and reinforce your vibrant culture. Some people will be deferential to your authority only because of your position if they grew up in a culture that trains people to be deferential to authority, and will find it hard to challenge you. Others will easily challenge your authority if they were raised in a low deference culture.

Engineering works best in an open information culture. This is a case where the tools that we use have a high impact on the culture. A clear example is the use of email and office docs to conduct the engineering process, because they tend to hide information. Using tools that encourage open information, such as topic-based text chat and wiki, will build an open information culture without people even thinking about it.

CHAPTER 6

Making Decisions

Decision-making is core to nearly all business and technical functions, and yet rarely discussed as a deliberate process to ensure positive outcomes. Different situations can demand varying involvements in making decisions which makes it hard to define a recipe that works everywhere, but at least we can build a framework that enables us to optimize a decision-making process for the problem at hand. If you do determine that you should enter a deep investigation into several options, be prepared to justify your approach as other managers may wonder why you are putting in effort to a non-coding exercise.

Ignorance and Risk

Nearly every kind of software development is an excursion into the unknown. If it weren't, we would just be rehashing the old work of others, and that doesn't add business value. If there is any single factor that threatens even the best laid programs, surely it would be our ignorance. Or more poignantly as Mark Twain explains: "It ain't what you don't know that gets you into trouble. It's what you know for sure that just ain't so."

What Twain is really talking about is assumptions. Many of the assumptions that we hold come from hard-won experiences and have great value when we apply them to future problems. But some of these

© David J. Asher 2024
D. J. Asher, *Mastering the Complex World of Software Management*,
https://doi.org/10.1007/979-8-8688-0841-8_6

assumptions don't hold when applied to new situations, and those can hurt our program. Trying to identify assumptions and then challenge them in some methodical way is the root of improving our decisions.

At the start of a program, we may think we have thoroughly defined a set of requirements and features, but we don't yet know the critical ones that we hadn't considered. We may think that we have conjured an optimal design, but we don't yet know the weaknesses that will be exposed upon testing and use. We may think that we committed to a reasonable delivery schedule, but we don't yet know all of the emergent problems that will derail it. We may think that we have secured all of the resources needed to complete the program on time, but we haven't yet observed the actual performance of those resources and where they will fall short.

It's important to be confident, but far more powerful to have the humility to recognize our own ignorance for all of these program aspects and so many more. The first step in addressing our ignorance is an evaluation of risk. This can be done by creating a risk register and tracking it throughout the life of its program. A risk register enumerates many kinds of risk, assesses the likelihood of each, quantifies any impacts, and suggests remediations. Some of the risks will be generic in nature, such as "we can't hire new staff fast enough." Some of the risks will be highly specific to the program, such as "our contractor fails to deliver their committed feature on time."

Pro tip: if you're unfamiliar with the process of cataloging risks, get some advice from your security team; it's their lifeblood. Creating a risk register should involve many team members because you need broad perspectives to identify as many risks as possible. It is the very act of trying to identify a set of risks that will open your eyes to so many failure paths in your program and to consider ways to compensate and significantly reduce the risks. It is often the management of risk, as much as good design and coding practices, that lead a program to successful outcomes.

Review and Improve

All of the aspects of feature determination, technical design, risk remediation, and so much else are the results of decisions. If we make good decisions, we should get a successful outcome. With each bad decision we reduce our chances.

If we never review our decisions in retrospect, how could we know whether our decisions were good or bad, and whether we have a good process for making decisions? So reviewing past decisions is a way to improve our odds of success in the future. We could simply consider the outcomes of past decisions, and declare a good outcome was the result of a good decision; however, that may not shed any light as to whether that decision was well made within a good process or was just lucky.

We can ask: was a decision the most likely to have a positive outcome given the information available at the time? It is quite possible to make a good decision that nonetheless has a bad outcome, because some factors that eventually caused failure were not knowable or even predictable at that time. This may be hard to judge given the hindsight benefit of knowing the outcome, and it may be difficult to reconstruct any knowledge then available and used to make the decision. Good record-keeping of meetings and decision events will be helpful.

Big and Little Decisions

How hard do you work to make better decisions? A one-size-fits-all approach may be just as bad as doing nothing, simply because some problems are small and others are large and you could waste a lot of time and effort analyzing things that will have little impact.

When the stakes are small, usually the preference for technology companies would be to move fast. Don't get caught in analysis paralysis just to fulfill a process; don't investigate options too deeply when you don't expect that information to alter the decision; don't spend effort looking for options when a perfectly acceptable one is readily available. If a decision is not hard to reverse, or the costs are low, or the outcome only has short-term impact, move quickly with just enough team buy-in to validate your assumptions.

As a problem may be recognized to have long-lasting impact, or involves a larger investment, or is foundational for many dependencies, or has the potential to drive costs into the future, or is nearly impossible to unwind – then it is begging to be more carefully scrutinized. The larger these knock-on costs may become, the deeper your investigation would be warranted, and possibly more people be involved in the decision process. In many cases of engineering, good decision-making is synonymous with technical investigation.

From the Gut

Some leaders profess that they are effective because their "gut" decision-making judgment is superior to others. They can face ambiguous or confusing situations and make the right call every time. They can make good decisions where critical information is missing and where other people are confused or stymied. What such people have is confidence; don't confuse that with skill in decision-making. And you have the power to learn how to make better decisions.

Let's say that someone is an acknowledged industry expert and still is a self-proclaimed gut decision-maker. The flaw in their approach is that every new problem is different than those before it, and their gut is not carefully considering how recent changes might affect outcomes. And if a person is making gut decisions but not coming from a position of expertise, then they are just trying to fool you to keep their position and will probably blame you later when failures happen. The flaw in their approach is that information that is missing may become knowable with modest effort, but they don't try to solve the thing they don't know because they are too confident. Any decision that incorporates more information will be better than a decision done in greater ignorance than is necessary.

Experience-based quick decisions can be helpful early in a decision-making process when you are assembling a set of options by making mini-decisions to eliminate some options. If you can quickly identify some critical reason why an option is unworkable, then you can eliminate it from further consideration and focus your efforts on the most promising options.

If a decision doesn't come from the gut, how can we be more methodical and achieve better decision outcomes? Let's dive into some approaches, starting with team decisions instead of an individual leader's decision.

Majority Voting

Let's assume a straightforward process, where a proposal with relevant background information and resolved unknowns is brought to a team, and the team uses a simple majority vote to make the approval decision. In many cases this may work just fine, but what happens when the voting result is a slight majority win?

Effectively, the team is split in their collective viewpoint, but the tie-breaking decision came down to one person's perspective. If you are wondering about the issue of having an even number of voters, this can be handled by having the team leader, or the proposal presenter, abstain from voting unless they are needed to break the tie. As a positive, notice how this process delegates decision-making from the leader in positional authority to the team, enabling team ownership of the decision.

However, consider how fragile this process is when a split happens. One person determined the outcome, but the team may not even be sure whether that person, or several of the voters, were considering seemingly unrelated factors or even may have a conflict of interest. Why did you have a team vote in the first place, instead of just letting the team leader decide? You were probably looking to get better results, and in this case it seems no more rational.

Consider further the impact on the team. After the decision, half of the team is in full agreement with the decision but half are in disagreement and are unhappy with the results. That disagreement could fester, such as those team members being less enthusiastic or productive, or even show conflict in future situations.

A majority-vote decision process may seem like the easiest or fairest way to arrive at a decision, but be careful because the likelihood of split decisions could prove to be the worst outcome for team dynamics and culture. The wisdom of the crowd doesn't apply when the crowd doesn't agree with itself.

Exposing Dissension

The discussion about majority voting presumed that all of the dissenting perspectives were exposed and considered, but that's a huge leap of faith because some people holding dissenting views may not take the initiative to express them. They may have doubts but be unsure of their position. And yet, it is exactly that minority viewpoint, or even one lone dissenter, that may hold the critical information needed to make the best decision. You could hold a round-robin discussion – go around the room and ask everyone, one at a time, to express any concerns, but that may not overcome the important dissenter's discomfort.

One way to handle this is to hold 1:1 discussions with team members, either before or after a team meeting. This allows anyone to ask probing questions, more deeply understand the subject matter, present alternative viewpoints, and raise objections that may not have been considered.

What's especially important is that team members can do this in a private environment where they should be more comfortable expressing their views, even if they have much less experience.

Another approach aligns with a culture of open information. Let's say that you are in a decision meeting, and once the background material and proposal have been presented, you ask all members to take an online survey. Make the survey anonymous, and ask people to enter whether they are inclined to support the proposal or not, list any compelling reasons to support it, and also list any objections or unseen consequences. Review the results together as a team, so now you have a common set of material for deeper discussion and have avoided any personal associations.

However you go about it, exposing dissension within the team may be the most important part of a decision-making process, since it exploits broader perspectives and deeper scrutiny.

Driving to Consensus

Consider that the American jury system of decision-making demands a unanimous verdict because majority voting wasn't sufficient to ensure reliable outcomes. A jury comes together as a team with a single shared goal. If the jury's goal was to make a decision and get out, then a majority vote would get the result quickly, every time, and you're done. But that's never the goal, rather it is to drive consensus, to argue all perspectives until agreement is reached with as much certainty as that group can muster, given the presented evidence.

If all decisions made in the business world required a unanimous verdict, we would never get work done. If we relied on the decisions of a single leader with positional authority, or used a majority voting approach, we may get quick decisions, but are unlikely to get decisions that fully considered as many challenges and consequences needed to make robust decisions. Can we do better?

It turns out that, when a team is faced with a set of options and sufficient details about the implementation costs and consequences of each, they often won't have difficulty coming to a consensus. At that point where the team is close to consensus, decision-making may devolve to more of a process of asking for any dissenting positions, and addressing those head-on with greater attention.

Let's recognize that, in any approach that doesn't require a unanimous verdict, some people will disagree with the decision. The healthiest culture is one that nurtures mutual respect for this condition. Leaders and those people in agreement with a decision should appreciate that some people are in disagreement, and that people holding dissenting perspectives weren't wrong, but were making important contributions. Those with dissenting perspectives should appreciate that business has to move forward, often quickly, and enjoying the benefit of being on a team means accepting some unpleasant decisions, and acting on those decisions positively and professionally.

RFC Process

The software industry has already developed a bottom-up consensus decision-making process known as Request for Comment (RFC), so why not borrow the idea for your own use? I have used this with a large team and found that it solved many problems with low effort and maintained high developer cohesion.

You don't need to get too sophisticated. Use an existing tool such as a ticketing system or wiki to maintain the documentation in a shared location, and define just a few document states such as Proposal, Draft, Rejected, and Approved. Have a conversation with your team about some basic rules and processes such as: anyone can submit an RFC; a first review must happen within two weeks of submission; permissions must be open and anyone can comment; at least six people must review the RFC and comments to get it to Draft; and so on. It all must work within your culture.

You can certainly use an RFC process to manage deep technical material such as protocols and APIs, but you can also use it to define just about any kind of process. People will get creative, and it's better to foster this creativity than to start setting exclusionary rules about what cannot be submitted.

Just Wait

One of the most useful tools to uncover dissension and manage disagreement is procrastination. Much maligned as laziness, it isn't always so. What if you don't need to make a decision for two weeks or even two days, then why force it today? By waiting, you allow time for new information to emerge that could affect the outcome, but especially, you allow for thinking to evolve.

Sometimes in the discussion process for a proposal, emotions can run high. People may feel all sorts of reactions, from apathy and wasting their time, to being personally contradicted or attacked. They may feel like they have a lot of time and intellectual commitment to an approach that is now being challenged, and their reaction is to defend the status quo. They may even shut down listening to information that is dissonant with their thinking. All of these are natural responses.

Forcing a decision at the moment when such a discussion happens, when team members are first hearing a proposal, when they are encountering some new or disruptive thinking, and when their own reactions may be highly defensive, is really the worst timing. So, just wait.

Give the team some time to reflect on the proposal, to explore some of the elements on their own, to hold discussions with other team members to clarify and align their thinking, and to sleep on it. There are some decision situations that clearly don't have the luxury of waiting, such as making a hiring decision where the overriding imperative is a fast and considerate response to the candidate. But whenever you determine that your decision can wait, let it.

Finding Bias

Someone is taking ownership of a proposal and asking for a decision. They may be the initiator, or may be acting on an assignment. Either way, their proposal will show bias. That's unavoidable, so the question is, how much bias is acceptable?

The key to fairness in any proposal is objective presentation of hurdles, costs, and especially, alternative approaches. These will show if the proposer has honestly looked at their proposal as one choice in a range of options. The more detailed, the more credible the proposal will appear to be, the easier it will be for teammates to evaluate. Even if some issues have only cursory treatment because the benefit/cost ratio of exploring them is too low to bother, it at least shows an open-minded consideration of the possibilities.

If a proposal is showing too much bias, most probably because it hasn't sufficiently considered the options, the presenter can be instructed to improve the proposal before entering the decision-making process, or can be assigned an associate to help work through the options and details. In any case, an independent review of a proposal prior to team presentation could save a huge amount of work that comes from subjecting a team to an incomplete proposal.

Disagreements

Because engineering teams are formed to achieve a common goal, and spend their working hours (and many sleep hours) steeped in the same set of problems and working approaches, most teams will trend toward a common perspective. This makes it easier for them to speak in shortcuts and yet convey a huge amount of understanding, and to dispatch smaller problems very quickly.

Most decisions that fall outside of the familiar domain of a team's understanding will likely raise disagreements as the team grapples with new concepts or encounters friction as they try to apply their old way of thinking to a new problem. Some of these disagreements may appear informally, for example when a new person joins the team and is able to see problems that the rest of the team couldn't see past their blind spot.

The second area of disagreement happens as soon as other teams are involved in the decision. Most engineering programs have multiple teams with inter-dependencies. Each of those teams exist precisely to encapsulate and insulate one problem domain from the others, therefore the expertise and perspective will be different between teams. When two teams are cooperating in a decision, or when an external team is directly impacted and therefore must be involved in the decision process, you can bet there will be more diversity of viewpoints. All of a sudden, a decision that seems great to one team can seem awful to another as the implementation costs or bad consequences land squarely on that other team. Driving consensus across teams is much harder, but much more critical to get right.

A team may find its decision on a problem to be perfect in all regards, but then presents the findings up the management chain and gets rejected. This usually happens because senior managers in an organization have a much broader perspective that individual contributors and lower level managers may be unable to see. For example, there could be budget consequences (no, you can't hire two new people for that project right now), or program conflicts (no, you can't do that because another team is already approved for a competing idea), or a fundamental difference in technical understanding of the problem. The senior manager wins, that's their job.

Make/Buy Decisions

One special case in decision-making is worth calling out: whether to write software at all versus acquiring most or all of it. It should come as no surprise that when you hire coders, they write code. So if you leave the decision to implement some functionality as acquired software versus custom coding, can you see that your coders have a conflict of interest?

Worse, their frame of reference may be so focused on coding that they won't even think to explore other opportunities to deliver functionality. Some engineers have the presumption that if they are writing code, it is innovative and has unique business value. That is often not the case if similar functionality is already available off-the-shelf; it's just an expression of their limited perspective. So it is up to technical leaders such as architects and managers to push the agenda for a make/buy decision when the conditions warrant it.

Make/buy isn't a binary decision; it's a continuum. In terms of coding effort, it can run from a full custom implementation, to modification of existing code, to full acquisition of code. In terms of where existing code might come from, again it's a continuum from a similar code base within the company, to an open source program, to a commercial product or service. And in terms of who creates or modifies code, again it's a continuum from employees to contractors to modifications by a software provider. So we have at least three dimensions of variation to consider just for figuring out how to get some code working.

If the work that you need done is totally original, great, go for it. But as a general rule, think about custom coding as a last resort. That is because if someone has already coded the functionality that you need, then you would not be innovating or delivering unique business value by rewriting that code. Unless – you determine that your own coders can deliver compelling advantages. Since your needs may vary somewhat from software that you can find off-the-shelf, it may take some work to figure out what options are available to you, and how they can be adapted to suit your needs. I have certainly managed cases where modifications to make existing code minimally useful would be so extensive that it is truly less expensive and more advantageous to write it all yourself.

Always bear in mind that every line of new code burdens its program with a lifetime of maintenance costs. It all adds up, and older programs can accrue outsize costs in customer support, bug fixes, refactoring, security patching, slow feature updates, and so on. So be deliberate when deciding to write code.

Weighing Factors

Making a decision assumes that you have options to consider, even if the options are a simple go/no-go decision. What's important to consider when evaluating options? That depends on the nature of the decision, of course. Let's focus on a particularly difficult class of decisions – problems of technology selection and engineering design approaches.

We can take an example design problem to work through the process: suppose that you need to build a public service exposing an API and hosted in a microservice that manages its own database. And remember, any one of these factors can be discovered to impose such an unworkable constraint that no further investigation is necessary for a particular option. If it's bad, then stop.

Precedents. The first consideration factor should be precedents. If your team, or nearby teams, have already built a bunch of similar microservices over several years, then just follow the established pattern. Even if you believe that a different database or some other design deviation might have an advantage, it's an extremely high threshold to prove that the burden of creating all sorts of duplication and exceptions would be ameliorated by the expected benefits. Sometimes we create a confusing architecture and operational mess simply by ignoring our own precedents or thinking that we are smarter than the last engineer.

Scale. Since the depth of a decision process depends on the scope of the problem, scale is the next priority to consider. If your service were to have limited exposure and low volume of usage we can consider the scale to be small. We would consider the scale to be large if it showed indicators such as many public customers, high transaction rates, or a huge data set. Effectively, large scale means that design decisions are very hard to change because of the weight of usage, and any mistakes are highly amplified in many troublesome ways.

Risk. Committing to develop software carries an execution risk: because it hasn't been developed before, the outcome could result in schedule delays, cost overruns, insufficient quality, or inadequate functionality as delivered. One of the key benefits of starting with off-the-shelf software is that it probably has been de-risked.

Cost. Different options can have a significant range of cost consequences, though it may be difficult to accurately compare the cost basis of some options. For example, an option may result in an increase in manual operations or customer support that fall under different budgets. Even if you can't reduce all options to currency equivalents, at least you can recognize the cost differences in a rough sense, such as small-medium-large estimation.

Time. Let's say two options are under consideration, where the option with a clear technical preference is estimated to take far longer to implement. If there is a schedule constraint, such as a customer contract deadline or a critical launch event at a conference, then the preferred option may not even be feasible if it can't confidently be delivered in time.

Licenses. If you will be relying on acquiring software as part of your solution, some open source or commercial software may have license restrictions that are unsuitable for your application or business. Licenses, particularly a General Public License (GPL) used for open source, usually can't be changed so this could be a deal-breaker. Read the fine print, and consult with your legal department.

Maintenance. Practically all software has some long-term cost to fix bugs and update it, therefore when you write new software you are burdening your organization with a lifetime of maintenance costs. And some software is much more expensive to maintain than others, so these costs should weigh in your decision.

Standards. Adherence to industry standards may be a critical factor in your business, such as supporting particular protocols, interfaces, or data formats. If one option has a known level of compliance it could be advantageous even if other costs are higher. Also be forewarned that if you are writing custom software and will require standards compliance, the effort is always harder than you think.

Resources. It is one aspect of project estimation to figure out the amount of resources, i.e., the number of programmers, that will be required. It is a very different aspect if some of those resources must possess a very particular technical expertise that is not currently available in your company or may even be hard to find in the industry. This kind of resource constraint could also impact the feasibility judgment of an option.

Intellectual Property. Software is often ignored when considering a company's IP position, particularly its trade secret value or patent value. But in some companies or industries, it is a critical consideration, and creating new unique and defensible IP may tilt the scales toward one option. Conversely, if an option is deemed to be infringing on someone else's IP then you'll probably want to stay clear of it.

Here's the Answer

There may be times when you are handed the decision to a design options problem from your supervisor or other leader such as a VP of Engineering or CTO. They may have knowledge about some of the evaluation factors that you are not aware of, or may be influenced by their preference for a vendor, or be responding to a major customer's input. Whatever the reason, you may be able to ask questions or challenge the answer, but be prepared to accept what you are given.

Recap

How you go about making decisions has a huge impact on your success rate, yet technology companies rarely discuss decision-making as a process, nor formalize it, nor hold managers accountable to following any kind of decision-making approach, nor review past decisions to encourage improvements. Yet all of this is quite achievable with a bit of thought and planning.

Our own ignorance is the biggest factor in making poor decisions, which can be overcome with a systematic exploration of risks, compiling risks into a risk register, evaluating contingencies for the more problematic risks, and tracking the risk register through the lifecycle of a program. Often a good decision can be made by understanding if there is an overwhelming risk rather than just looking at possible benefits and costs.

There can be several ways to make a decision within a team. Delegating decisions to the team members, rather than yourself "making a call" as a manager, will build trust and encourage confidence in each individual. When the team as a whole should be involved in a decision, it is worthwhile to try driving the team to a consensus position. Procrastination can be your friend, as there often is no point in making a decision too early, allowing for better information inputs to evolve over time. We all approach decisions from a position of bias, which is where the diverse perspectives of a team can lead to a better decision. Not everyone will agree with all decisions, but in a healthy team people will accept team decisions even if they don't like it, and that includes the manager accepting team decisions. There are specific kinds of decisions that are worth building a framework to help resolve, where one important example is make-buy decisions for software functionality.

When a decision has low impact or is not hard to reverse, it may not be worth spending much effort on making the decision. But if the decision leads to high costs, high impacts throughout a program, or is hard to reverse, then it should be worthy of deeper analysis and a more formalized approach. Some of the weighing factors for big technology decisions include: precedents, scale, risk, cost, time, licenses, maintenance, standards, resources, and intellectual property.

CHAPTER 7

Program Governance

Engineers get work done through "programs" and "projects," but these are loosely defined constructs and can take many different forms, sometimes even used interchangeably. Here we'll use these terms as follows:

- **Program:** A commitment to build or operate something that delivers significant business value, which can either have a defined ending or may function perpetually.

- **Project:** A smaller component of work that is typically part of a program and has a defined deliverable and ending.

- **Portfolio:** A collection of programs that share business objectives.

- **Governance:** The set of rules, processes, and structure for managing programs to success, inclusive of individual projects, and sometimes collected within portfolios.

Managing programs is a completely different work dimension than managing people and teams, but sometimes the same Engineering Manager is responsible for all of these, with or without help from Program Managers and Project Managers. There are many professional societies dedicated to Project Management across a number of industries; they seem to consider Program Management to be a specialization within

© David J. Asher 2024
D. J. Asher, *Mastering the Complex World of Software Management*,
https://doi.org/10.1007/979-8-8688-0841-8_7

Project Management. As a result there is a lot of great training material on Project Management, so let's focus on the relationship between Program Management and Software Engineering.

Program Leadership

Programs are often complex work structures involving multiple teams across a variety of disciplines. Whether a particular program incorporates non-engineering functions is a decision for each organization; there isn't a right answer. Who is the leader? You may imagine that multiple functions would imply multiple leaders and maybe some level of cooperation or leadership teaming, but that doesn't answer the question.

Think about leadership from the perspective of an executive, who may make the statement: "give me one throat to choke!" Okay, maybe not so violent, but the point is that an executive needs one person who is responsible for truth in reporting, will be held accountable for all costs and deliverables, and that will answer the call whenever the executive has a need. So there may not be a right answer, but surely the wrong answer has any number other than one.

The "executive" in this context may not be a single person. A program may have a number of stakeholders, perhaps even outside of your department or chain of command. If you are in the leadership of a program, you must be clear about identifying all stakeholders and attending to their information needs. Hearsay may leak to a stakeholder from time to time, and as it travels from person to person, it may get distorted. You don't want your stakeholders taking action on hearsay, so it's important to report your status often enough and with enough fidelity to maintain yourself as the source of truth about your program.

When programs are complex enough to cross department boundaries, you start to see org charts with "dotted lines." Normally an org chart is drawn as a set of boxes representing managers and solid lines representing reporting relationships. A dotted line represents a person having a second reporting relationship, a kind of second boss, where the relationship is narrow and defined for a specific purpose. For example, as an Engineering Manager you may be reporting to your engineering supervisor for all personnel needs, but have a dotted line relationship with a Program Manager for all deliverables in that program, and your own supervisor may not even be a stakeholder.

Partner to Lead

As discussed in Chapter 4, "Leading Teams," being an Engineering Manager in the hierarchy can be an isolating situation, and more emphatically so when playing a dual role as a Program Manager. When a program is small and mostly contained within a manager's engineering teams, this arrangement can be a natural fit and easily workable. It isn't wrong to assign a single person to be responsible for both engineering teams and a large and complex program; however, it should be recognized as a heavy load and demanding a broad skill set.

I have found the most effective way to handle these dual-role situations in a big program is by building a partnership with other leaders. If you are the Engineering Manager, reach out to people in other roles, such as a Program Manager, Project Manager, or Product Manager to join you in partnership. A small partnership of just two or three leaders can be immensely more robust and powerful than a single leader, and helps to relieve some of the effects of hierarchical isolation.

Among your partnership of leaders, make clear the delineations in primary responsibility for various aspects of the program. I say "primary" because each of the leaders should be able to provide backup for the others when the primary is absent or just too overloaded to handle something. This partnership doesn't need to be a formal construct, but it is important to have a common understanding that there is shared responsibility even though there is still only "one throat to choke" as far as the chain of command goes.

When working with everyone else, it may be helpful to have some explicit guidelines about your divisions of responsibilities; however, since you are able to back each other up in many situations, most people will either figure out who to talk to, or just talk to the most convenient or familiar person. It's then up to your partnership to keep in constant communication and dispatch any issues to each other as they arise.

Making a Delivery Commitment

The whole point of a program is to get work done, and your responsibility as the Engineering Manager is to deliver that work. What defines the work, who does it, and when does it get delivered? These are the essential elements of the commitment you must make when agreeing to lead a program. Usually these are evaluated at a project level because that is where the real work of software development happens. A program may then aggregate and coordinate across multiple projects.

For software development, a typical process looks like this: the desired outcome is defined with a Product Requirements Document (PRD) or a Statement of Work (SOW); technical interpretation of the deliverable is defined with an Engineering or Functional Specification; a Development Plan validates the effort and resources needed and estimates a delivery date; a Risk Register gathers and addresses possible misfortunes; and sometimes other planning documents are used such as a Test Plan, User Interface Definition, and so forth. Let's get into some of the details.

What Defines the Work?

Names may change, and formats and details may vary, but engineering work is defined by requirements and specification. Requirements are what the organization is asking you to do. You cannot (and should not) make a commitment solely based on requirements because you haven't vetted them.

In many organizations, a Product Manager writes a Product Requirements Document (PRD) which expresses a vision that may be completely reasonable but may also stray from the reality that you're familiar with. But once committed to paper, you can all review it and align all its aspirations against technical and organizational feasibility. Similar principles apply to a Statement of Work (SOW) in the case of contracted development, as well as situations involving internal programs such as IT, manufacturing, operations, or other enterprise services; here, we'll broadly use the term PRD. If you don't have some equivalent to a Product Manager writing a PRD, then you are in for an unpredictable outcome.

The PRD should articulate *what* should be built but not be prescriptive in *how* to build it. Your response to the PRD is an Engineering Specification (or Functional Specification) which expresses what you actually intend to build, with all of the technical details that you have confidence can be delivered. Once the owner of the PRD has reviewed the Engineering Specification and agreed that you are describing a reasonable technical implementation of the PRD, then you have agreement on the work definition and at that point, it's the Engineering Specification that defines the delivery, not the PRD.

Who Does It?

Your Engineering Specification is most useful if you have made a set of effort projections for implementing the spec. Usually this is a bottom-up process of estimating the individual efforts at the lower levels of functionality across an entire project. The estimations will be rough because high accuracy is nearly impossible.

It's popular to use t-shirt sizing for each area of functionality to be estimated (e.g., XS-S-M-L-XL) but at some point a conversion to real-world effort must be made, using units such as person-months. The units need to express time and resources, with enough granularity to be meaningful. The total effort is the sum of all individual work items, and if it is way beyond a reasonable scope of time and resources, then you're in a loop going back to the PRD and trying to negotiate what to remove.

There is another dimension that has an impact on the work estimates: who is working on each task? It's critical because some software engineers are far more productive than others, but even two equivalently skilled engineers may have very different time requirements for completing tasks if one is unfamiliar with some important aspect and must take time to learn it. At the phase where you are estimating future work, you're not making actual work assignments yet, but you can use a productivity model based on the average performers in your team, and also account for the learning time needed to compensate for skills gaps.

Once you have your final effort projection, it needs to reflect an achievable staffing level, whether it's the resources that you currently have assigned, or whether it's a new or expanded team that needs to be hired.

How Big Is the Effort?

Requirements and schedule and resources are often described as a project triad that must stay in equilibrium. If you add requirements, then either resources or schedule must increase to compensate. If you shorten the schedule, then you must add resources or remove requirements to compensate. If you drop resources and hold requirements constant, then you must extend the schedule to compensate.

The calendar time to make a delivery must be derived from your effort projection. If the required level of resources isn't immediately available, then you need to add calendar time to account for getting funded and assembling the team. If the team will only be 50% productive because of time off and meetings and unrelated project maintenance, then you need to expand the effort by 2x and adjust for weekends and holidays to determine the span of calendar time.

Arriving at the total calendar time required, you want to add some buffer because there are always surprises or things that you didn't estimate so well. How much buffer? The best answer is to base it on the track record of past performance from your team, but it's never precise, which is exactly the point. The second best answer is to base it on the size of the known but unsolved problems. Let's say that within a project you must write a new algorithm to predict future demand for your product and have no idea how to go about that, then that's a pretty big unsolved problem.

The more work that you can do up-front to bring some clarity to the needed solution will enable you to make better work estimates and reduce your buffer. You should be honest with yourself once all of this information is assembled and reviewed. If you have low confidence in your team's ability to deliver full functionality at high quality on the commitment date, you may have more planning work to do. But you also can't get into a cycle of refusing to commit until you have near certainty. There will be risks and you are getting paid the big bucks to make a commitment, balanced between identified risks and the time and money to deliver.

When Does It Get Delivered?

Taken together, your Engineering Specification, effort projection, and resource allocation constitute your Development Plan and should be sufficient to make a delivery commitment. Some engineers argue about whether they should deliver to a target date, or deliver whenever they determine their software has sufficient functionality and quality to ship. Let's settle this: *Your job as a program leader is to ship on your committed delivery date. Always.*

The reason is simple: the world works on a calendar. Whether it's a customer expectation, a contractual obligation, an unveiling at a trade show, a marketing launch program, a dependency needed by another team, or just because the CEO said so – there is a world out there waiting for your software and the consequences of any delay can range from inconvenient to catastrophic.

Software development is a discovery process, so it is almost guaranteed that your Development Plan will be wrong. New features may be introduced during development, the user experience turns out to be awkward, the team is spending way too long chasing down bugs, performance is way too slow and needs to be optimized, and on and on. The project seems to shape-shift as you make progress.

Therefore when you uncover a problem that adds work, shouldn't you push back your delivery schedule? *No!* Your competency as a program leader is not because you can make deliveries when everything goes right, it's because you can make course corrections and still keep your commitments even when things go wrong.

But Wait, Aren't We Agile?

Sure, you can use Agile methodologies for development, but jumping into an implementation phase to be "agile" with minimal planning doesn't allow for building a confident commitment up front, nor any predictability in a delivery date. As the practitioners say: you aren't agile because you're fast, you become fast because you're agile. And the way Agile methodologies become predictable is to resolve unknown factors early in the process.

In other words, if you don't put care into up-front planning, you really don't have a solid foundation on which to claim that you know anything about how long it will take, and how many resources, to deliver. You may also be leaving large gaps in understanding between your engineering team and the product requirements because they haven't been surfaced and resolved through the process of writing an Engineering Specification. So do your homework.

In fact, if you think about Agile methodologies extending across the entire lifecycle of a project, then you can use techniques such as a time-bound sprint and task backlog to write the Engineering Specification and create all of the effort estimates needed to build your Development Plan. If you find that you are having trouble converging on a Development Plan, that's a strong signal that you aren't ready to commit, or should be taking a different approach.

When Do We Consider Risks?

Consider a stock prospectus or corporate annual report; maybe you gloss over it but there is always a substantial compendium of risks. These are intended to inform you *before* you make an investment decision. Or look at the directions for any medication which likewise catalogs a set of risks intended for you to read *before* taking that medication.

And so it is with a software development commitment. Every stakeholder should be demanding and reviewing your risk register *before* they make the final decision that your Development Plan and proposed commitment is satisfactory and ready for investment. This gives them a chance to challenge your understanding of particular risks and get satisfied that you will professionally navigate any risk that materializes and threatens the program.

If you are taking your commitment seriously, as if your job depends on it, then you also want to build the risk register prior to presenting your Development Plan. While you are exploring risks, you will be discovering improvements to the plan itself, and every one of these will increase the likelihood of successfully meeting your commitment.

Does the Order of Implementation Matter?

Very often a Development Plan has multiple mini-commitments within the broader program. There may be a prototype needed to build confidence in the architecture, several milestones defined in order to demonstrate progress, interim deliverables to resolve dependencies with other teams, alpha and beta releases that are offered to select customers, and so on. Each of these mini-commitments needs to be rationalized along the timeline of the Development Plan, where all needed functionality and sufficient quality assurance are completed in time for these deliverables.

But another important element of the development sequence is resolving unknowns. If there are projects and tasks that have significant unsolved problems, waiting for the end of the development sequence will leave you with no maneuvering room to manage the unexpected. The general rule for successfully meeting commitments on software development is to look for unsolved problems and dispatch them as early as possible in the lifecycle of the project.

When Should You Perform System Testing?

Early. Often. Any thoughts of serialized build-it-then-test-it flew out the window with pure waterfall development methods. The information you need about development quality is critical for keeping schedules on track, even if the testing process itself seems to be consuming too much time and resources. System testing becomes the most powerful tool for tracking development progress and validating that what you intend to build is actually what you are building.

Metrics and Reporting

Imagine that you are authorized to start implementation of your Development Plan and ten months later, two weeks before the big deadline, you notify your stakeholders that your project will be delayed by six weeks. That breaks the golden rule: never surprise your boss. If you hadn't uncovered the delay until just before you reported it, the accountability and consequences are still on you, and rightly so, because it's your job to be keenly aware of your team tracking to the Development Plan at any moment. The most effective way to understand development progress is to define a set of metrics and then report regularly on those metrics.

It turns out that a set of mini-commitment milestones may be useful not only for delivering to outsiders, but also to pace your development effort. It will behoove you to insert internal development milestones solely for your team's benefit, as the accomplishment of each milestone builds confidence in your plan and serves as an early warning signal for trouble.

Internal milestones reinforce the Agile principle of always having a demonstrable system, and the most fundamental metric you can track is the satisfactory completion of milestones. Each missed milestone is an event that signals the development team may be experiencing turbulence and needs corrective attention immediately. Don't let missed milestones fester because time losses accrue quickly and each one makes future recovery so much harder.

Resource metrics may be needed if team building is going on while the Development Plan is under way. Your metric would indicate your success rate in filling job openings, and level of tracking against your hiring plan. Often a hiring plan has some critical, hard-to-fill positions and those need to be highlighted separately.

Quality metrics are also an important aspect for project tracking. You should have quality metrics from your bug tracking system, such as the rate of discovering new bugs, the rate of closing bugs, the backlog level of old bugs, and some kind of prioritization between minor bugs and bugs that have critical impact. Many build systems also scan source code and produce quality metrics which you can track and report on, and use their scanning results to make corrections.

Some Agile methodologies have useful project tracking capabilities as a by-product. For example, if you are using feature points to define work tasks, you can use a burn-down chart to track the rate of closing the feature points over sprints – or it may reveal the rate that your team isn't able to close them at a satisfactory rate.

A good metrics report on a program really has two parts: the quantitative metrics results that are described numerically or in a chart, and a story about the failure cases and what you are doing to correct them.

Delivery and Reflection

Getting through a Development Plan and successfully delivering is a big deal. The team can be tired from stress or long hours, especially near the finish line. So go ahead and celebrate your achievement.

A helpful behavior is to lead a retrospective session after each project completion. In a normally functioning Agile environment, there will be regular team retrospectives, possibly after the completion of every sprint, but these are highly targeted on mechanics of the development process and usually work on low-level details. A retrospective after a project completion is elevated to the scope of the whole project. The team should be recognizing the challenges faced and praise its successful reactions. Most important is to address and tackle the episodes that could have been handled more effectively, even if the outcome was positive.

Self-critical introspection and brainstorming will lead to ideas for improvement and the team's realization of how much control they can have over the development process. These are the best ways for a team to advance its competency, project after project.

Business Team

Consider how any organization operates strategically and ensures that complex work is assigned and coordinated across its management hierarchy – it has an executive team comprising the top leader from each major functional area of the organization. They meet regularly as a team, raise significant issues, share status and progress, make proposals for improvements and innovations, deal with crises, define initiatives and implement them as individuals or subgroups, and take direction from the CEO and President.

Once an organization gets large enough to operate at the scale of multiple programs, this same governing structure can have enormous value when applied to programs or portfolios. That's the concept behind a Business Team. The problem that a Business Team is addressing is: who is running the business?

Typically, a company has a number of people filling roles that are necessary to conduct the business of a portfolio – finance, customer support, marketing, sales, operations, product, maybe legal or other functions. However, they often aren't coordinated. For example, if a company is directing one of its product lines to increase its revenues, they have options to add features, or change pricing, or launch a marketing campaign, or acquire a competitor. Which will produce the best results?

When the responsibility for running the business is diffused among several people that don't regularly coordinate, it's hard to solve a problem like this in an optimal way. Or perhaps some options don't even get considered because the leader assigned to the problem has a bias because of their background and position.

A Business Team collects representatives from various functional areas that have relevance to a program or portfolio. These may be at the level of senior managers, directors, or VPs, but what's important is that they have the authority to make decisions on behalf of their functional area. A Business Team needs a chair, and often that person would be the one who is most motivated to grow revenues and profits which is typically a Product Manager, although it could be more administrative in nature like a Program Manager.

The Business Team chair should be accountable for achieving the goals of the program, and functions like the chair of any Executive Committee or Board of Directors: call meetings, set agendas, negotiate goals, propose strategy, assign tasks, track progress, report to senior management, and manage emergent issues. In group format, they use their diverse set of resources to solve problems quickly and efficiently. They coordinate with individuals in between meetings to ensure that the business of the program stays on track.

Creating Business Teams is a robust way to scale-up an organization, because it's too hard for a single top-level executive team to manage the business details for many programs, and a single program owner doesn't have enough perspective and resources to actually run a business.

Customer Advisory Board

The following mostly pertains to companies that sell to enterprise customers.

Many organizations assemble a Board of Advisors comprising outside talent in order to inject a perspective that is deep in industry experience yet unbiased by internal factors. When a program or portfolio has this kind of need, they sometimes convene a Customer Advisory Board, which is typically an annual event. A CAB is like a mini conference, where large and strategic customers send a representative such as a CIO or IT manager.

The representatives of the CAB get some benefits, such as contributing to the direction of their vendor, networking with other industry players, and maybe a little golf. As an enterprise vendor, you would run various sessions and workshops where the participants can offer their perspectives on aspects of your business and future directions that are under consideration.

It is complex and expensive to put together an event such as a CAB; however, the insights gained from unfiltered feedback can be invaluable for setting a profitable strategy and avoiding costly mistakes.

Vendor Relations

A program will have two major external interfaces, the vendors that supply software, equipment, and services to your team, and customers that consume the final results of your program. An organization will typically have a number of well-developed touch points for customers, such as Account Managers and a technical support team. However, for vendors there may not be a formal interface so you have to take it on, and it's usually handled at the program level. It's a good assignment for a Business Team.

Some vendor relationships are simple and transactional, but even so, establishing the transaction may still require that you evaluate alternatives, try to get the best pricing, negotiate any options or services such as long-term support, get cleared through corporate security standards, and arrange acquisition, training, customization, and anything else needed to make use of the vendor's offering. You may find that other parts of your company, like the IT department, are helpful and willing to manage the contract, especially since they are very skilled at that.

When vendor relationships move to the strategic level, you will find that you may need to coordinate with other parts of the organization that also use the vendor. You may also find that the vendor has an account team that is focusing on you. It can be great when they help with technical problems and throw merch at you, but can be a bit tiring when you are the object of their sales efforts.

Recap

The major unit of work in an organization that delivers business value is a project, which may exist in the larger context of a long-lived program or portfolio of multiple programs. Sometimes an Engineering Manager is called upon to be the owner of a project fully responsible for its delivery, or sometimes that ownership falls on a Program Manager or other leader. In any case, governance of a program will be stronger when led by a partnership; however, senior leadership should identify a single throat to choke when it comes to accountability.

When you are accepting responsibility for the delivery of a project, you are making a commitment. It is in your own best interests to have confidence that you can complete a delivery with the requested functionality, resources, and schedule. You can really only have confidence if you are able to estimate the work, beginning with a thorough understanding of the functionality. Since you can't spend forever making perfect estimates, the best shortcut is to look for the aspects that you understand least or that pose the greatest risk, and focus your exploration efforts to better your understanding of those. You will keep reporting progress throughout development and delivery of your project, never hiding the bad news.

When a program is large and complex, it may be unclear who is actually running the business and so it warrants a formal governance structure such as a Business Team. Mid-level or senior leaders across company functions are collected and empowered to make decisions directly at Business Team meetings. This structure enables a program to make things happen quickly when the right people are in the room. Another approach to assist a large program is a Customer Advisory Board which is often practiced by enterprise vendors and enables rich and honest feedback about your products and customer relationships.

CHAPTER 8

Software Development

There are only three steps to successfully manage a software development team:

1. Hire exceptional people.

2. Challenge them.

3. Get out of their way.

The rest is detail, which we will get into.

Getting to a Process

It will be helpful to define a few important terms in the context of software project management. There are lots of helpful and conflicting definitions that you can find online, but the following should suit our purposes.

Framework: A framework is a way to organize a problem space, in this case software project management, by showing its most important components in a logical way and explaining how the components relate to each other and how they are useful when operating in the problem space. A framework presents helpful concepts but isn't specific enough to be directly applied to software development.

Methodology: A methodology introduces a set of tools, techniques, and interworking methods according to a framework, such that a practitioner can use the methodology to understand, modify, and deploy successful work patterns.

© David J. Asher 2024
D. J. Asher, *Mastering the Complex World of Software Management*,
https://doi.org/10.1007/979-8-8688-0841-8_8

Model: The software development industry has converged around several models of methodology. While there can be variations, most align under one of these: Waterfall, V-model, Spiral, Iterative, and Agile. Since several studies indicate the adoption of Agile at over 60% of projects, we will mostly focus on that when it's important to be specific.

Process: A process reduces a methodology into very specific rituals and required artifacts that a team can exercise on a continual basis in order to achieve predictable outcomes with a reasonably efficient use of resources.

Frameworks and methodologies tend to be widely proselytized, whereas processes have unique adaptations for every situation and to some extent, every team. It is a process that we utilize every day in our software development, and it is the frameworks and methodologies that we use as guidelines to help us define our processes.

Reflecting the engineering side of software engineering, software leaders would almost never start with a blank page for a methodology, not when you can be building on a proven body of knowledge. There is a mountain of industry experience and wisdom embodied in each methodology, and that is the most stable and productive starting point for any new project.

Agilebut

I have asked many people at different companies the simple question, "what software development methodology do you use?" The answer invariably starts out, "we use Agile, but..." So I've come to think of modern software development as "Agilebut." I am not discounting the use of other methodologies, but this sense of "it almost fits" in Agile Methodology is a useful principle that can be applied to the others.

The first team I managed that made a deliberate conversion from a Waterfall Process to Agile Scrum was quite successful in achieving its goal of a predictable delivery schedule while maintaining great quality. Actually, I was a Product Manager at the time, but had helped write our Software Development Lifecycle (SDLC) and was quite familiar with the engineers. Moving faster wasn't a goal, but they achieved that, too. About a year into this experiment, our group of involved managers held a debrief session with some of the engineering staff, since we were eager to copy this success onto other teams.

Our engineers shared this insight: they didn't believe that any particular methodology would have made a significant difference over any other. The game-changers for the team were the deeper way in which they were now communicating, involving Quality Assurance (QA) and other roles early in the process, and actually producing more documentation while getting the work done faster. They suggested that any methodology giving them the rituals to build these behaviors would also have been successful. In the spirit of this realization, this book will not get prescriptive about any particular software development methodology but will get into the details about the kinds of behaviors that lead to dynamic teams and successful outcomes.

What Agilebut means is that any methodology must be adapted to be useful, and those adaptations result in somewhat unique processes. The process to develop software under contract to a single customer will look quite different than does product development. A team pulling maintenance tasks from an issues backlog and measured by their speed of work has distinct needs from a team inventing algorithms and measured by the competitive advantage they create. Software developed within a regulated industry has additional layers of process and constraints than does general use software such as office productivity apps. Requirements that are heavy in user interfaces, say mobile apps or voice assistants, will drive a far different rhythm of development than real-time systems such as industrial controls or data storage devices. No one size could possibly fit all of that.

When considering different methodologies for your team and how you will make adaptations for your situation, be deliberate and not pedagogical. The foundation of various Agile Methodologies is a set of principles known as the Manifesto for Agile Software Development and then has been evolved into a series of methodologies that emphasize their usefulness in particular situations, for example Agile Scrum and Kanban being two of the most well known and practiced. These methodologies need to be considered in the context of a product, team, organization, and culture, and then formulated as a set of processes, rituals, and artifacts. If some aspect isn't working for you, change it and adapt. If your process isn't a living thing, it's probably broken.

Agile at Scale

If your software development is entirely contained in a single small team, there isn't much for us to talk about. Your specs can be loose, your process barely defined, and you can make so many mistakes that with a few corrections you'll keep going and be just fine.

But for a large or high growth project, one of the biggest challenges is the way that it often starts with such informalities because there is no reason to burden a small fast-moving project with process overhead, but then fails to catch up with process maturity when new teams are added. All the problems pile up when scaling up.

Typical symptoms of a high-growth project with lagging process maturity would be: some teams failing to meet delivery commitments, high bug rates and inability to solve all of the bugs, bottlenecks driving slow performance, misuse of APIs and interfaces, constantly changing database schemas, poor documentation, confused onboarding for new entrants, a customer support backlog that grows faster than tickets can be resolved, and misunderstood requirements leading to wrong features or bloated code as programmers keep cranking even if they aren't sure what they should be doing. You may even observe malaise, frustration, and cynicism amongst the engineers – or, they are just too busy to cause trouble. A bit of process in the right places can help with many of these issues.

Most development methodologies really focus on the abstraction of how a single team should behave, but don't address the challenges of scaling up. Specific techniques to address scaling have become popular such as scrum-of-scrum meetings for coordinating work across teams, but that is just one dimension of many scaling problems. Some methodologies have arisen to meet the broader need, such as the Scaled Agile Framework (SAFe). A customer driving a large contract, a government agency for example, may dictate a standard for you to use, such as ISO/IEC 12207.

In all of these situations, process adaptation is required. The work to adapt a methodology for a single team is greatly magnified when considering a growing project or performing a process clean-up of a large organization. Generally, there will be teams in different phases of development, and facing a wide variety of software tasks, such that creating a rigid standard for all teams to follow is probably unworkable. Scaling up Agile processes requires not only adaptation into a particular organization but also some degree of flexibility for each team.

Retrospectives

Since there is no out-of-the-box software process that can be applied directly and work satisfactorily in all situations, the methodology that you choose must be reduced to a process that works for you, and the more thoughtfully, the better the results. But even with the best considered adaptations some aspects won't work so well, and conditions change over time that beg the process to be improved, else the process itself will put a drag on the team. So if you accept the premise that different approaches can be workable but must be adapted and need course corrections over time, then the process itself should anticipate and accommodate change.

To achieve this ability to evolve, the single most important ritual in any software development process is engaging in retrospective sessions. If something is broken, it can be fixed, but only once it's identified and the team is amenable to changing its process. What kind of process changes are we talking about? *Anything.* There should be nothing that is off-limits to discuss. A retrospective collects practitioners, preferably the whole team, and asks them to review things that worked well, things that didn't, figure out the factors that caused unsatisfactory outcomes, and propose process changes to raise performance.

You can find online a bunch of tools for guiding retrospective sessions but the simplest is a whiteboard or some sticky notes on a blank wall, and the most important is a shame-free and open-minded attitude from all of the participants. It may take a few rounds before people become accustomed to the style of a retrospective and trusting of each other. Retrospectives need to encourage an environment where everyone feels safe to ask questions, empowered to make suggestions, and energized to volunteer for improvement projects. Sometimes the presence of a manager can be intimidating or can be stimulating, so I've found that scheduling some retrospectives with and without the team manager is a helpful approach.

There can be small retros and large retros. Small retros happen more frequently, focus on finer details, and result in incremental change. A good team habit is building a retro into the sprint cycle for review of the sprint just completed. This allows the team to reflect on process elements while relevant events are still fresh in everyone's minds and involves the specifics of situations rather than gauzy memories. Retro sessions can scale up, like after a project is completed, so that a team can reflect on the entire experience and consider big and impactful changes. Especially for these larger retros, your role as a manager is to challenge the team to think more deeply, inject tough questions, and force consideration of events the team may be more comfortable forgetting.

Time Bandits

If you are managing a software development team, then I already know this about you: you don't have enough resources to get all of the demanded work done in the expected time frame, and also your software development process is loaded with wasted time. So allow me to suggest that, before escalating your complaints and trying to get more resources, you might try to reduce some of the time wasted by your own inefficient methods. Any time recovered by making efficiency improvements accrues right back to your team's total work capacity, so you can get more done.

Engineers have a notorious tolerance for accepting low productivity because, they assume, things are just the way things are and they have no agency to change it. Maybe your code build operation takes a half-hour, or your deployment pipelines fail 30% of the time, or code check-ins can't get quickly completed because code reviewers are too busy and don't prioritize it, or setting up a dev or test environment can take hours.

This time banditry causes inefficiency because these blocks of time are too short for a developer to switch context and regain productivity, yet if you multiply by the number of times in a day the waste is repeated, and multiply again for each developer, you should realize that a significant amount of your team's work capacity is wasted. And if any of these time wastes are inherent in common processes shared across an organization, the productivity losses add up, too. You just haven't been able to see it because you haven't been adding it up. Ah, I hear you saying, "yeah but I don't own those operations, so-and-so's team handles that and I can't change it!" News Flash: wrong, it is your responsibility. If you see something broken, fix it, or help the owner to fix it. That benefits your team, and everyone else.

You'll notice that the above examples are pure software development concerns. If you widen your perspective to include meetings and other non-coding activities, you may find even more opportunities to recover lost capacity, and slay the time bandits.

Software Development Lifecycle

A Software Development Lifecycle (SDLC) is the documented process for your organization's software development. Defining an SDLC doesn't guarantee that all software development will have successful outcomes, but in reducing the variation and chaos from each team behaving differently and making up their own process, an SDLC will make it much more likely that your teams will succeed. As long as the SDLC isn't too encumbered or hard to follow.

You can find templates online for an SDLC according to the methodology and model that you are using, and that may be a great starting point. An SDLC will divide work into phases, for example a Waterfall model will progress sequentially through Requirements → Design → Development → Testing → Deployment → Maintenance. The most important aspects of the SDLC are explaining the work expected during each phase, and especially being specific about artifacts produced. A phase of development is understood to be making progress, or completing, because certain articles of code or documentation artifacts can be reviewed.

In a Waterfall model, phases are understood to be distinct and work progresses to the next phase when the expected artifacts are reviewed and approved. Taking a different approach, an Agile model will encourage overlapping phases, for example engaging the Testing Phase as early as possible during the Development Phase. Just because an Agile process may not require a stringent demarcation between phases does not mean that artifacts and reviews aren't needed.

The activity of writing an SDLC is a terrific way for an organization to encourage discussions about the way they want to work, and to consider how different models of development can be applied to your situation to achieve the greatest impact. I encourage you to think specifically. For example, when working with teams about to embark on a new program based on Microservices Architecture, we created an SDLC that detailed phases of API development, how the API progresses through microservice development, and all of the artifacts that are needed along the way. This SDLC for Microservices proved to be very helpful for our teams to always know what was expected of them and to produce consistent results between teams.

You may be thinking that processes like SDLC are heavy and slow an organization more than they help. Process definition is an essential feature of a thriving and maturing software organization, but does not need to be at odds with productivity or innovation. Quite the opposite; a well-crafted process will enable your engineers to understand what is expected of them without the effort of making up something new every time. These processes are also far more effective at the organization level than the team level, because that would allow senior managers to have a consistent view of all activities, and enable individual contributors to transfer between teams and still understand how to work.

Robust Architecture

Performance, of your system as well as your team, is first and foremost enabled by its architecture. What is meant by architecture? It is the decomposition of the system into high-level components, the level of interdependency and volume of communication between these components, the extent of data sharing among components, choices to build or buy each component, and the myriad selections of tools and technologies. When you work on a well architected system, problems and costs are reduced, and life is just plain better.

An architecture may seem good when its program starts off, but any cracks in the foundation will be exposed under the stress of growth and scaling. Under sufficient scaling, certainly within one or two orders of magnitude, even the most robust architecture will break, but at least a robust architecture will last longer and yield greater benefits along the way.

What usually leads to poor architectural choices is lack of perspective and jumping to conclusions before considering options. Most engineers bring their personal experiences when tackling a new problem, or sometimes a non-personal experience they read in a book or found in other media. If a set of engineers is under time pressure, or just a bit under-curious, they will follow their experience bias and take the short path to what they believe to be the best answers, because what worked before should work again, case closed.

This is where an architect can make a huge difference. An architect carries many diverse experiences giving them so much material to draw from, with each experience informing benefits and drawbacks learned from solving problems and living with their real consequences. Combining these experiences with an elevated curiosity and sharp critical thinking skills, a good architect will spot weaknesses, even if just a hunch, and then track them down. Their next step is to investigate any problems more deeply, survey the industry for known solutions, and make an architectural decision based on thorough problem understanding and a set of options to explore.

While it helps to have this kind of architect on staff, you may be able to succeed without them, but you will need to challenge your engineers. That can begin with asking simple questions. *Why did you pick this language for implementation?* If they can't give a reasoned answer other than *it works and we know it*, give them an assignment. *Why are you using this protocol for messaging? Why are you separating these functions into different modules?* And so on. Answering simple questions will demand that their architectural choices are exposed and made explicit by considering problems more deeply and exploring options to solve them.

There is an approach among Agile practitioners known as Emergent Architecture, which recognizes the inevitability of problem discovery and the usefulness of system evolution by incremental improvements. In true Agile spirit, get hands-on coding immediately so that you always have something working and can build on those successes. That's all good, but it can also lead to an architecture emerging that is far from optimal because some technical decisions – or lack of decisions – get baked in very early on and are hard to change, simply because they were not given sufficient thought before coding.

An approach that can more predictably lead to a robust architecture is to first draft an architecture at a high level, with just enough detail to ensure that all requirements can be accommodated. Based on that, look for the unknowns, the pieces of your new puzzle that carry high risk, and put priority to those. You can resolve your lack of understanding by looking for industry examples that have solved similar problems, and building a proof-of-concept (PoC) implementation. Where Emergent Architecture might have you first building the most foundational aspects, this approach would have you first coding the riskiest parts, or at least investigating them. Then once you have more complete knowledge of the problems facing you, you can refine your draft architecture and at that point, being well informed, start coding.

Microservices

If you have been developing software in the last ten years, the odds are good that you have either been using a Microservices Architecture, or your manager asked why you aren't. There are a few factors relating to building microservices that are important for a manager to know. The following are hard-won experiences from building a large scale microservices platform from scratch with a newly formed team.

How big should each microservice be, and how many microservices should a team be responsible for? Our team made the creation of a new microservice to be brain-dead easy. Literally there was a microservice creation web page that anyone in the company could use. Enter the name for your service, a few options like coding language and database, click submit, and presto! A new microservice was minted that you could start developing with immediately. Whether it was for testing or development or internal corporate use or fooling around, we didn't care. Microservices for everyone!

You might think that, having such an easy route to creating new microservices, our production system would be swimming in a sea of them, but that was not the case. As easy as it was to create a new one, getting a microservice into production was a very rigorous and time-consuming process, plus you can add the persistent overhead of monitoring and administration of a production service. For any service where security, stability, and scaling are high priorities, this kind of production rigor should be the case.

Our high production threshold put back pressure on the development teams. When considering some new functionality, they may think that from a perspective of architectural purity a new microservice should be created, but when considering work aspects and overheads, they often made a pragmatic decision to push new functionality into an existing microservice. Therefore each team tended to be responsible for one or a few microservices, and we found that number never proliferated, and microservice size was self-regulating.

The decoupling between teams enabled by a Microservices Architecture is a huge advantage over traditional, "monolith," architectures, but there are consequences, of course. The most direct consequence is inter-service communication cost, which we can further break down into the cost of security, the cost of observability, and the cost of transmission. These costs arise because the inter-functional communications of traditional architectures, typically function calls and message passing within a server, are private and cheap, but become network traffic in the case of microservices.

The microservice cost of security should be clear: what was private communications within a process or between processes within a server becomes much easier to snoop or spoof when it becomes network traffic. This forces extra security measures on communications such as encryption and packet signing, and the architectural features to prove that your security framework is in fact secure and not illusory.

The cost of observability also increases because network traffic is much more difficult to observe – it should be fully encrypted, right? So let's say that an external API call triggers your microservice which in turn has to call other microservices and so on. How do you know where a call failed, or is showing high response latency? Tracing packages have filled this gap so that you can follow these call flows, but these produce a huge volume of traces, just like log collection does.

Communication cost between microservices increases, first because of the overheads of using network protocols and encryption, and secondarily from any growth in call volume. As your growing set of interacting microservices handles higher traffic rates, the inter-service communication cost can rise exponentially relative to the rate of overall service growth. When it's operating at a small level this cost won't be noticed, but once your service hits success, you may literally get the bill.

There is a credo amongst many Microservice Architecture adherents that teams should act independently and make the best technology selections for themselves. We found this approach can work beautifully and it can work chaotically. For one example, our teams started out coding mostly in Java and Python. Once one team encountered performance issues and recast their microservice in golang, it caught fire and quickly became the default language. No top-down management dictate was necessary to achieve alignment or even special hiring or training, the teams just did it. Yet when these teams were left to their own selection of database technology, it turned into a huge mess that forced us to build a database-as-a-service capability that enforced data consistency and administration, to everyone's benefit.

Good Coding

So far in this chapter, we have been considering the formalities of developing software at an organizational level, but ultimately delivering great software depends on the individual craft of coding. Good code is not just a matter of taste. It is the efficiency of our coding which leads to higher productivity and therefore lower cost and higher profits and bigger bonuses, and the innovation of the code that we write which leads to competitive advantage and greater revenues and growth, and the quality of the code that we write which leads to a safer and more stable and more enjoyable result for our customers and end users.

One way to achieve product quality is beating mediocre code into submission through an exhausting cycle of testing and fixing, or, we can write quality into our code from the start. If you accept an assignment where a large body of code already exists and has demonstrated a high volume of bugs, you may find that you have no choice but an exhausting cycle of test and fix. But if you are creating new code, it's up to you as a manager to ensure the conditions where all software engineers will be writing high quality code from the start. We'll take this approach and spend the rest of this chapter on the craft of coding.

Your target should be zero bugs. Seriously, zero. If it isn't, then please answer, *what is the acceptable level of bugs that you are targeting?* Because an Engineering Manager is responsible for the quality of the code their team produces, they must also be responsible for the coding techniques the engineers use, and their culture of quality.

A universal challenge in team coding is that the person that wrote some code may not be the person assigned to fix or modify it, and this becomes more true over time as any piece of code often outlives the tenure of its original developer. Writing good code is as much of a respectful consideration for other coders as it is for your own productivity and quality results, and writing code that is readable is one of the most important quality aspects of team coding. If you are a Software Manager, mentoring good coding hygiene is a critical part of your team's success and even career advancement.

The foundation of team coding is setting expectations for what good code looks like, which is usually done through a Coding Style Guide. Following a style guide will ensure consistency from the simplest issues like variable naming and formatting, to recommended usage of complicated language constructs. Having a Coding Style Guide is also an essential element of performing code reviews, because it provides the reviewers with a standard which helps to enforce consistency and quality across an organization. But here you are in luck. Not only can you find great examples of coding style guides online, but Google has published its set of style guides for the most popular languages, and they are available to you on GitHub.

Your Enemy: Code Complexity

Code executes first in the mind of the developer. Complex code results in bugs because it surpasses our mind's ability to fully understand its machinations. Ever since Edsger Dijkstra wrote his March 1968 letter to the editor of the Communications of the ACM, *Go To Statement Considered Harmful*, the software community has had increasing awareness that messy and complex coding matters a great deal toward the resulting code quality. As a community of practitioners we seem to have gotten past *goto*, but there are still subtle ways that we are creating random access and convoluted logic paths.

The most readable code and least likely to have bugs is linear in its logic and this is the essence of reducing code complexity. Any branch in code execution, where the code might subsequently follow either of two paths depending on some conditions, marks a place where the coder needs to keep in mind what happens under all branching conditions and trace its consequences through multiple places in the code. Therefore,

155

reducing complexity often means reducing branching. Think of the simplest code as having a linear sequence of instructions without branching.

Consider a single in-line statement that performs *if/then/else*, also known as the ternary conditional operator:

```
answer = (check_input > threshold) ? get_bigger() : get_
smaller()
```

If you were to express the above in-line statement as higher complexity code, you would have a conditional expression followed by *then{}* and *else{}* blocks, which forces the code reader to follow the branching logic in multiple places. By moving the *then{}* block to the *get_bigger()* function and the *else{}* block to the *get_smaller()* function and writing an in-line statement, the complexity has been hidden. All of the branching logic is encapsulated and your mind, as you try to mentally execute the code in and around it, can simply reduce this to comprehending an assignment, then move to the next line of code. It's a low-complexity way to express branching logic.

For the most part, a block of *if/then* conditional code would have a low-complexity branching logic and isn't that difficult for a reader to comprehend – if the code is kept short and simple. The readability challenge happens when the *then{}* block gets long, or the statement requires an *else{}* code block.

```
if (conditional_logic_goes_here)
then {
   // block of code, keep it simple and it's easy to follow
}
else {
   // once we introduce this block of code, the reader has
   to follow
   // the path of execution in two places
}
```

156

The challenge to a code reader is that an *else{}* block forces understanding of two possible code paths. As the code blocks get longer, it gets harder to associate the executing code with the test condition, and fully understand all side effects of those code blocks. It's like a Schrödinger's cat problem right there in your code.

The *if\then* code branching complexity problem starts exploding when *if\then* statements are nested within *then{}* or *else{}* code blocks. By nesting, the coder may have been simply following the conditional pattern of the real-world problem, so they think they are being true to the problem by encoding that complexity as code branches. But because nested *if\then* statements become devilishly hard to mentally execute and therefore likely to introduce bugs, we in fact aren't being true to the problem at all. I once found a segment of production code nested seventeen levels deep, and yes, it is very smart people that do this kind of thing.

Your Friend: Boolean Algebra

A far more reliable approach is to encode any conditional expressions within boolean algebra and attach those directly to each code block. You may be thinking: *Yuk, I'm a coder, I don't do algebra anymore!* Well, it's not hard once you practice a little. Working out the original problem as a set of boolean variables and equations forces you to be more explicit about conditions and more likely to catch conditions that you couldn't see when using code branching logic. Consider a typical but still fairly simple code nesting pattern:

```
if (outer_truth) {
  if (inner_truth) {
    // inner code here
  }
    // outer code here
}
```

```
else {
  // isn't outer truth
}
```

which become less complex when cast as boolean algebra instead of code branching:

```
if (outer_truth && inner_truth) {
  // inner code here
}
if (outer_truth && !inner_truth) {
  // outer code here
}
if (!outer_truth) {
  // isn't outer code
}
```

This pattern has the readability benefit of the logic tests appearing in close proximity to their respective blocks of conditional code which is an easier mental association, plus it becomes possible to insert other code between the conditional blocks without increasing complexity. Coders tend to avoid this pattern because it requires evaluating the same variable multiple times, but consider that this evaluation is just a simple check on a variable's state; it's the cheapest code to perform. And I beseech you, even if this code is somehow less efficient, as a general rule it is far better to write simple and readable code than it is to save a few CPU cycles.

Now consider if we cast the same logic into several boolean variables:

```
is_inner_truth = outer_truth && inner_truth
is_outer_truth = outer_truth && !inner_truth
is_no_truth = !outer_truth
if (is_inner_truth) {
  // inner code here
}
```

```
if (is_outer_truth) {
  // outer code here
}
if (is_no_truth) {
  // isn't outer code
}
```

Now you have a set of variables that can be tracked with debuggers or log statements, making observability and debugging much easier, plus you gain the possibility of reusing the variables to observe state within your code.

Once a set of boolean variables is defined, it becomes much more clear that code can be written as a linear set of simple *if*|*then* code blocks or even a *switch* statement, without resorting to code complexity and nesting. The conditions for executing a code block are visually obvious, and not a side effect from execution branching further up in the code. This approach is especially helpful with improving readability for languages that use indentation to demarcate code blocks (looking at you, Python).

Defensive Coding

A best practice in writing any function is to first check the validity of all input variables. You don't want to be handling a pointer or reference variable that is null, an array index that is out of bounds, a user text input that contains malicious injection code, an expected number that is actually text, a function reference to call on exit that doesn't exist, and so on.

Even if you know the calling code perfectly well, and completely understand that this function can't possibly be called with a null object reference, an unexpected error somewhere else in the code can shatter your assumption, and tends to do that at the worst possible time. So think of these error checks as self-protection of your function, a defensive mechanism to prevent the unexpected error from cascading.

A second reason to be thorough in validating all function inputs is that your function may be used by another coder that recognizes the usefulness of your function, and because code reuse is next to godliness, diligently calls your code but in an unexpected way. Your input validity checks may have prevented that second code instance from introducing a bug.

Perhaps most importantly, getting in the habit of thoroughly checking all of the input variables to a function encourages thinking more deeply about the use of your function, can reveal unexpected bad inputs or even bad patterns between multiple variables, and expose possible ways your function may be used in the future so it can be better generalized.

When we stopped using random code jumps with *goto* statements and adopted code blocks with *BEGIN|END* or *{}* or whatever, a natural result was to be friendly to the compiler and always write complete code blocks, allowing only a single exit point at the end of each function. This makes pedagogical sense and looks clean. Except this is exactly the dogma that led to complex code execution paths. As anti-civilization as the *goto* statement may be, a return statement especially on an error condition is a special case that should be considered and befriended. Let's take the situation where input variables are checked for validity at the start of a function.

For example, say that some function has three input validity checks to be performed, with a negative result of each check being that no further processing can take place. While dogma suggests that we should still carry forward the code path toward the clean exit at the end of the function, in terms of readability, this is burdening subsequent code with the outcome of the test. Worse, a logic error in complex code branching could cause subsequent code to execute when that was never intended.

This case of insidious creeping code complexity is easily resolved by using a *return* statement as soon as any error condition is determined, which can yield a linear sequence of code statements that do not read as complex.

```
function(a,b,c)
{
  if (is_bad_input(a)) return ERROR_STATE_ONE
  if (is_bad_input(b)) return ERROR_STATE_TWO
  if (is_bad_input(c)) return ERROR_STATE_THREE
  // now write the code that the function needs to perform
}
```

Because this code now has a linear structure, complexity has been reduced and it's easier to read and understand.

Random Access

Most coders have readily accepted the premise that random access to bits of code via *goto* statements will often yield unexpected results, i.e., bugs. The same principle applies to data structures, but this concept seems less well accepted. When you are storing data in an array and you have full control to randomly access any element at any time, it may be too much flexibility where some small error can cause things to go sideways.

For example, say you need to add an element to the end of an array. In some cases, a new array may need to be allocated with elements copied, and then the last element found, new element written, length of the array updated – you know the drill. Or, just a *push()* call will do it all when using a stack structure instead of an array.

Every time that you write some code to perform basic access functions to an array is an opportunity for a bug. All of the code that is ever needed to write and access array elements in an orderly fashion has already been written, fully debugged and ready for you to simply make a method call. Pretty much any modern language or coding framework has these data structures already, so making use of them will reduce bugs. In some languages (e.g., JavaScript), an array may be defined as all-powerful and incorporating the functionality of a stack or a queue, in which case forgive my disparagement of arrays, but please still use the data manipulation methods provided instead of random access algorithms that you write.

You have all found nasty bugs in the boundary conditions of a *for|next* loop. Very often a *for|next* loop is scanning across an array or a string, or in some way hunting for an answer, or trying to process all elements. It is the boundary conditions, however, that are the trickiest to code and test for robustness. You may be quite confident that your *for|next* loop was coded correctly, except that millions of experiences inform us that we often get it wrong. Our code attempts to access an element outside of the data set boundary and of course it wasn't supposed to, but that's what a bug is. Your own experience should confirm this.

Native Resources

In most languages, the whole boundary condition situation of a *for|next* loop is avoided by using an iterator. The risky work has been done for you. The reason that you were using a *for|next* loop may have been to search for something, or to perform an operation such as a splice, once the location is found. Your language or framework is also giving you these higher-level functions to search and splice and such, so use them to reduce bugs. The same holds for strings as well as arrays and most data structures.

The language or framework that you are using has many built-in features for rapidly building functionality and relieving you of writing code, and therefore you get fewer bugs. Don't be thinking that you are going to write routines that are faster and less buggy than those provided by your language or framework; it's better to rely on this work that has already been optimized and debugged.

Take one example that you probably don't like: regular expressions (regex). Many of the custom functions that you have been building for string parsing can be quickly and reliably encoded as regex. I hear you whining, "the regex specifiers are strange, hard to read, and can also be buggy." All true. But writing regex statements gets easier the more you use it, and they are generally not hard to test since you can easily throw a set of input test strings at them. A regex statement will be far more compact and reliable than a string parsing routine that you write for a custom purpose.

A dictionary object is another example, which may go by different names in various frameworks. When you consider a dictionary object as a quick lookup mechanism for information, all kinds of problems can be solved with them, instead of writing code. Similarly a key:value store can be used as an algorithmic building-block that obviates the need to write a lot of code.

Exceptions

*<HERETICAL>*One of the worst programming features foisted on developers is exception handling.*</HERETICAL>*

The views contained herein are completely my own and you may strongly disagree, but I'm writing the book. With that out of the way, let's get into it.

GRIPE #1: Error handling should be a fundamental aspect of any good coding practice, not an exception to good coding. You are more likely to increase bugs if you are not fully understanding the possible error cases while writing code. An exception might make perfectly good sense when your computer throws a hardware fault, but isn't giving you any new capability when it's just software logic gone wrong.

GRIPE #2: Most exception handling facilities such as *try|catch* blocks shred any sense of code readability and force code execution to suddenly jump to a different place.

GRIPE #3: By jerking the code execution path, you may lose context that could be important for troubleshooting.

GRIPE #4: In the exception handler, you may lose the opportunity to respond to the error as a perfectly normal code behavior.

GRIPE #5: For an end user, the result of an exception is usually some disorientating behavior and a thoroughly unhelpful message.

What to do? When you make a function call, you should be expecting it to return with expressive error details, and then you should handle all of the error cases. When working with dependent code that throws exceptions where you have no choice but to implement an exception handler, a useful pattern is to make those calls within a function that simply wraps an exception handler and then returns useful error information.

Code Comments

If comments aren't code, why would we be including comments in a discussion about code quality? Because code readability is one the biggest factors affecting code quality, and the quality of code comments has a big impact on readability.

As pointed out earlier, if code executes first in the mind of the developer, then comments are there to explain why that code exists and how it works in case that isn't obvious. It's for the human code readers. When comments are excessive and gratuitous, they get in the way of clearly seeing the code execution path and operations, so it's harder to spot bugs. Just like coding style guides, there are many commenting style guides with all manner of recommendations, so adopting one could help improve your code readability.

One important case of commenting is automated documentation generators. For some situations such as producing APIs this can be enormously helpful. But sometimes you look at code and see a bunch of empty doc generator comment sections. That's usually a sign that a team established a convention to apply automatic doc generation to all code, but that doesn't actually produce the documentation, or produces it but never references it. Mess up your code and then get no benefit? Don't do this.

Performance Optimization

Performance seems to be top of the agenda for many developers, who often think that their code is great if it's fast, as opposed to highly readable or very low in bugs. The trouble is, from the customers' or company's perspectives, performance may not be the highest priority relative to others, such as time needed to write code, testability, cost of execution, code size, support costs, and so on. A common coder behavior is to optimize for faster performance before it has been proven that code needs to be more performant. Highly optimized code tends to be buggier code. Maybe that's a law of the universe, because it seems impossible to get around it.

In many software situations, the single most important coding criteria is to get the coding done quickly and without bugs, therefore the best first-pass at writing code should be to exploit the highest-level framework facility, or someone else's code, that gets this job done. If the code is then tested and performance is not shown to be a problem, you're done, don't optimize, and don't let your team spend time optimizing something that hasn't proven to be non-performant.

Even within real-time systems and signal processing, it is often the case that much of a program doesn't need to be optimized because it doesn't run frequently in the core computation path. So if you do head down the path of optimizing code, be careful to understand which components of the code are actually contributing to lower performance and optimize only those.

Recap

This chapter delves into some critical aspects of managing software development for those who need more guidance than this fundamental recipe for success: hire exceptional people; challenge them; get out of their way. When you find yourself starting a software development project from scratch, or needing to mature a fledgling, it's important to understand the conceptual foundation of framework, methodology, model, and process, because it is a unique process for your team that you will need to craft from well-known models, methodologies, and frameworks.

Agile has become the most popular methodology with a number of useful models that you can tap, but you will need to put some work into adapting it for your situation, and to be especially vigilant for scaling up your software development process as your program grows. Two of the more effective means for keeping an Agile process on track is regularly holding retrospective sessions, and looking for the time bandits that cause your team to lose productivity. All of this can be captured in a Software Development Lifecycle document and used by team members to keep their practices close to the intended process.

If you get everything else right but miss on architecture, your software will suffer when scaling and require extra cost to maintain it and compensate for lower performance and lower quality customer experiences. A seasoned Architect can help establish a strong architecture from the get-go, but even without that a Software Manager can frame a set of problems and challenge their engineers to help them build a robust foundation. A very popular architectural style is known as microservices, which can be very successful at decoupling teams so they can work independently; however, achieving scale can introduce unexpected costs and technical hurdles.

The remainder of the chapter espouses some essential tenets of coding craft, because once you've assembled a great team, developing great software depends on process, architecture, and coding. One of the most important tenets is reducing complexity in code, where we often introduce complexity unwittingly with excessive code branching and nesting. We also do ourselves no good when building custom code while our selected language or coding framework supplies optimized and tested functions and data structures.

CHAPTER 9

Software Quality

There is plenty of great source material to understand software testing per se, but from a Software Manager's perspective it's helpful to think about the quality of human–computer interactions and the meaning of bugs through real experiences. In this chapter, we'll take a very expansive view of quality, especially relating to the kinds of fuzzy problems that are more recently being tackled with Artificial Intelligence.

A Beautiful Example

While working on a software upgrade to the avionics package for Grumman's A6 Intruder aircraft, I was looking at the design for the back-seat bombardier/navigator control panel. What sprang to my mind was an infant's busy board toy with big colorful buttons and knobs and toggles and such, all different things to twiddle, making no cohesive sense to anyone older than a toddler. The B/N panel had different interaction devices even when their intended function was similar. Every switch, button, and knob was oversized and had a unique shape. It was a visual mish-mash that wasn't comporting with any modern UI design sense. At first glance, kinda ugly, it was.

Then realizing that military gear couldn't be designed by accident, there must be a method to this madness. So consider that the B/N would be masked and maybe wearing gloves, and needing to make a split-second action within a highly tense situation, physically stressed, possibly

© David J. Asher 2024
D. J. Asher, *Mastering the Complex World of Software Management*, https://doi.org/10.1007/979-8-8688-0841-8_9

confusing, and may not even be able to direct their visual attention to the panel. And making a mistake about deploying a bomb does not allow for a do-over.

So what were the designers after? There would be no aesthetic criteria, because no user or buyer would care about that. Functionality that encouraged use of exactly the right controller without making a mistake was paramount. All of a sudden, this user interface design became beautiful to me as it was perfectly functional, meeting all performance requirements, and not meeting any contrived requirements. And how did this design come to be? That was a job for Human Factors Engineers.

Before we had disciplines of User Experience Designers and User Interface Engineers, there was Human Factors: the application of what we know about people, their abilities, characteristics, and limitations to the design of equipment they use, environments in which they function, and jobs they perform – all following a rigorous and scientific process.

Consider some of the complex human/machine systems that were arising from the last mid-century, such as space exploration, power generation, air traffic control, and military equipment. In terms of design criteria, aesthetics would play practically no role, but performance (taking the exact intended action), safety (avoiding any mistakes), and information processing (understanding a situation accurately) would be the highest. Even cost considerations would be further down the priority list.

When a Human Factors Engineer encounters a new design challenge, they can draw from a huge base of research and prior design knowledge. Meeting a new design challenge isn't an inspiration or a conjuring, but the application of this enormous understanding of working examples toward the new problem. When they don't have high confidence in the prior art, new research may be necessary. There is no guessing; just good engineering.

How would you know whether a user interface design is a good one, or poses challenges to some users? If you see a debate forming where there isn't an obviously superior approach to a user interface, engineers and designers could get caught arguing, taking sides on an issue that comes down to their preference but perhaps no real data to back up their position. In many software situations, it isn't hard to find out the best alternative among several user interface approaches. Often this can be done inexpensively with a prototype, which may make the superiority of one approach clear once it's reduced to a real experience. Or the prototype can be presented to a focus group, so at least a set of unbiased reactions can help to guide designers to the right answer.

Even better, an increasingly popular UI approach is A/B testing, a highly dynamic design process where two versions of the user interface are released at the same time as a kind of contest. Effectively this becomes a real live experiment in the market. May the best interface win! Like any experiment, there should be a hypothesis about possible outcomes, with instrumentation, data collection, and results analysis to understand the evidence. Why argue about a UI in theory when you can test alternatives and prove the better one?

System Bugs and Ambiguity

When systems become large and complex, the toughest bugs may not be coding errors.

In 1988 the guided missile cruiser USS Vincennes was on patrol in the Persian Gulf, as Iran Air flight 655 took off from Bandar Abbas on a scheduled, short straight flight to Dubai, passing over the Vincennes. The takeoff flight pattern could be interpreted as a hostile threat, given the Iran-Iraq war waging around them. The ship's captain attempted radio contact but got no response, then fired two SM-2MR missiles, killing all 290 crew and passengers. Of course the captain did not know this was a commercial airliner, but he was working with ambiguous information, and there was recent context influencing his decision to open fire.

A year earlier, the frigate USS Stark was on patrol in the Gulf when a jet took off from Iraq and flew directly toward the Stark. The ship captain attempted radio contact but got no response, and initially took no defensive action. The Iraqi aircraft launched two Exocet missiles at the Stark, leading to an explosion and fire that killed 37 sailors and wounded 21. Surely that's not an error that the captain of the Vincennes wanted to repeat.

In both of these events, the captains attempted to communicate with the unidentified craft over radio and check their identity or issue a warning, but since that failed in both cases, the captains were left with ambiguity. These complex systems are intended to work accurately when information is complete, but become less reliable as information ambiguity increases. While there are so many details and complexities to these events, the situations had similarities in their broad story lines yet ended in opposite actions being taken, both resulting in tragedy.

I was a systems analyst on the software team that produced the Command and Control System software for Oliver Hazard Perry class frigates including the USS Stark. In US Navy acceptance testing, the software was cited for a handful of minor bugs, a remarkably strong performance even for mission critical software like naval C&C systems. Enormous efforts are expended in specifying requirements for these systems, building and testing them, and further confirming their correctness and effectiveness through realistic scenarios and exercises.

The investigations following the Stark and Vincennes events didn't really focus on technology failures and system bugs were not targeted as the cause of failures, but still the question gnaws at the analyst's mind: isn't a system failure of this magnitude a quality failure, the result of a bug?

We software practitioners and systems engineers often think of a bug as an error in calculation or logic, a clinical discrepancy between a system's specification or documentation and its observed behavior under test. That may be a sufficient definition for a system that primarily performs a computing function such as data storage or financial processing. But many of our computer systems are integrated with sensors and actuators to enable them to work in real-time human-world applications.

When you are designing software and working through the details of a user interface, how much do you really consider the unpredictable reactions of a user, the surprise actions you don't expect them to take as a result of ambiguous and unexpected inputs, and the ways in which the context that your application is used may be quite different than what you intended?

With people in the loop, we need to think of software quality and bugs more broadly. Public confidence and trust in the systems that we build will depend on the way that engineers define correctness, and to the extent that we can incorporate the unpredictability of humans and real-world situations when designing and testing.

An Untestable Problem

Are all systems testable? Even if we hit the holy grail of 100% code coverage in our tests, can we achieve near-perfect quality control of our software?

Before Artificial Intelligence was viable, the most sophisticated approach to pull signal from noise was the Kalman Filter, an optimal estimation algorithm that works by comparing measurements against a model of expected behavior, and it found particular success in sensor processing applications. With my master's degree freshly minted in signal processing, I snagged a position designing such a Kalman Filter.

On day one, my manager handed me this problem: The sensor is in orbit with a deep infrared pixelated view of Earth. Targets will launch, and you have two minutes to identify them and start tracking them. Up to 20 targets in a cluster, closely spaced in time and location. The signal-to-noise ratio is low and up to three targets per pixel. He handed me the current work from scientists that considered their solution to be theoretically perfect, a FORTRAN program that took 24 hours to process a two minute scenario and never even converged to an answer. Please fix this.

My first attack was proving Kalman's theorem for myself, for as the physicist Richard Feynman expressed, *what I cannot create I do not understand.* I then began to deconstruct the problem as a split-brain computer scientist and physicist. I used graph data structures to store and process information rather than large matrices; optimized calculations by taking advantage of symmetry in the data; recognized the computer architecture problem that large matrix operations were constantly flushing the CPU cache and slowing down calculations instead of speeding them up; analyzed the covariance elements that were unnecessary or more likely to add noise than information; and upended then refined the physical models. I built a simulator to generate views from the sensor's perspective, ran scenarios and measured results, and also the prime contractor had engineers running their own scenarios to check the quality of my work.

After a year, the results were a two-minute scenario converging in 20 minutes with 95% accuracy. Interpretation: the two-minute deadline is critical because the boost phase of an intercontinental missile is about two minutes of very bright, slow, mostly vertical travel, after which it becomes dark and hypersonic and very much more difficult to find, so boost-phase tracking could provide a head start for defensive measures. Twenty minutes of run-time was within the useful performance range because it was a simulation running on a fairly slow general purpose computer. Ninety-five percent accuracy meant that one in 20 targets may get dropped from tracking. There goes Baltimore.

For a very simple scenario like a few loosely spaced targets, there isn't a need for the level of sophistication I was applying to the problem; it only held value in a crowded field of targets. At this point, I was mulling over the fact that all of my work was applicable only when the world was having a really bad day, so I was challenged by a very fundamental question of whether I was building something that was at all useful. That question became easy to answer since Congress didn't invest further, but other compelling questions emerged: Could the system be tested? And to whatever extent it may be tested, could it be trusted?

As engineers, we are accustomed to seeing a technical gap and trying to close it with incremental improvements or invention. We could keep testing an algorithm under simulation and eventually get to better and better outcomes. Maybe even 100% code test coverage. Even if you could get there, all of the automated testing in the world does not address an algorithm's performance against unpredictable conditions. And today's compelling problems are about algorithms and large data sets operating in a real world of unexpected conditions.

I raise the above extreme example to demonstrate that some systems cannot bridge this testing gap, in large part because the situation where the system is most badly needed to perform may be rare. Or hopefully in some cases, will never occur.

Coming full circle to Artificial Intelligence, you may notice an analogy between my example and some systems that are coming into production. Sure, we can build a system that accepts sensor input and generates actions in real time. You can always build an algorithm to arrive at an answer. In some cases, an AI system like a voice assistant in your kitchen may almost always yield some kind of results because erroneous responses can simply be ignored or laughed at. In critical cases, like self-driving cars or medical diagnosis, erroneous responses can be deadly.

Tales from the Debugger of Last Resort

The most powerful debugging tool is the gray stuff between your ears.

As much as we may test and try to instill as much quality as possible into the systems that we build, bugs happen and solving them quickly is part of the quality cycle. Following are several vignettes of bugs that seemed to come to me when others threw up their hands. These demonstrate some important aspects of bug hunting:

- Debugging is about finding the mechanism that explains why your code went awry and often the code fix is trivial after the mechanism is revealed.

- In some cases I was a manager, which shows that a fresh pair of eyes can be very helpful, even if they are the eyes of a manager.

- Code debugging tools weren't needed, and sometimes when you see an engineer spinning their gears with a debugger and not making progress, it's better to have them put down the debugger and start reasoning.

- In none of these cases did I have any familiarity with the relevant area of code where the fault lied so that isn't a requirement for assigning someone to find a bug.

- As engineers we usually require a problem to be reproducible before we take our time to start debugging, but sometimes we can make progress without it.

- Sometimes the bug isn't a coding error, but it still may be the responsibility of a software engineer to figure out some kind of fix for it.

- Some error conditions are so weird that it's nearly impossible for a software developer, and even a quality engineer, to consider that special case during testing.

Best Approximations Aren't Close Enough

When executing a test scenario on a target tracking console, a target is placed at 10 km due North and when that happens, its position unexpectedly flips to 10 km due South. Although the scenario may be contrived, having any target shifted to an obviously wrong position is a really bad bug. The programmers in the team were certain that we didn't have a line of code that says "if a target is at 10 km due North, move it." So they handed the problem to an analyst.

I suspected a math problem, since I agreed with the programmers that there wouldn't be any code logic to explain it. Geographic processing relies on trigonometry functions, especially sine and cosine, to convert between cartesian and polar coordinate systems. Here it is important to know how computers perform math. Basic operations like addition and multiplication are executed precisely in CPU hardware, but higher level math such as transcendental functions and derivatives are approximations calculated from the math primitives using techniques such as polynomial curve matching. For sine functions that method is called a Taylor series expansion, which is a polynomial with coefficients defined so that its curve very closely matches the sine over one (or a half) cycle. But what does *close* mean when trying to get one curve to match another?

Because the goal is numerical accuracy, the coefficients are determined as a set that produces the smallest distortion when compared with a true sine function. Mathematical purity was the priority, not practical usage in the real world. The problem with this approach is that the lowest distortion curve will not have a perfect zero crossing, i.e., $sine(0)$ must be 0. That was the case in the math library that we were using, and the result is that a position that is just a tiny bit positive can turn negative, and vice versa. Some sine functions solve this by forcing $sin(x) = x$ for very small values of x. Our library didn't work this way, so the solution was to slightly modify the coefficients to guarantee a clean zero crossing, favoring the real world over minimal distortion.

A Bug in Silicon

I was working on the low-level BIOS firmware for laptops, and was handed a customer prototype that used the brand-new Pentium-class CPU from Intel. So my first step was to take the existing source code that ran perfectly on a previous generation i486 computer, rebuild it, and test it on the prototype. As expected, everything worked well. Except, attempting to run the BIOS setup utility immediately triggered a crash. I figured that would be a quite unpleasant debugging task so I ignored it and went about other work.

A couple of weeks later, Paul from our sales team came up to me and asked if I knew anything about this crash on Pentium systems. I said, "Oh yeah, I saw that a few weeks ago and have been avoiding it, but figuring to get to it soon. Is there a problem?" He explained that this bug has popped up in other systems, Intel was blaming the chipset vendor, the chipset vendor was blaming Intel, customers were blocked by this problem and hollering, the whole thing was blowing up. Help! Realizing that Paul was previously a BIOS engineer and knew his way around the code better than I did, I told him to pull up a chair and let's team it.

I said, "there's one difference between this setup utility and all of the other functions that are working, so let's start there." Paul said, "right, it's triggered with an interrupt rather than a function call." So that's an easy test, we replaced the interrupt with a function call, and the setup utility was invoked perfectly. I proposed that this should be an easy fix, we just need to correct the corresponding entry in the Interrupt Descriptor Table, for some reason it must need a different value for Pentium chips. Paul explained, not so fast, those particular interrupt vectors are initialized by CPU microcode, not BIOS software. If that's right, we're looking at a CPU hardware bug.

To prove it, we were able to set up BIOS code that forced correct values into those interrupt vectors, and that worked. So there were several weeks of companies blaming each other without ever diagnosing the problem, which I was able to solve with help from an account manager in a few minutes, just by following the clues.

A Bug in Documentation

A customer of our high-density telecom gateway board was attempting to enable a special feature called Circuit Emulation Services (CES) which conveys digital content over a T1/E1 communications trunk to support modern cellphone traffic. The customer couldn't get it to work as expected. Our product was making use of a special-purpose switching chip, so the customer called the chip vendor who confirmed that this feature should be working. Our customer escalated their complaint, and since they wouldn't be able to satisfy their own customer commitments, they were threatening a lawsuit. So I was handed the problem.

I first checked with our lead engineers, and they were certain that this chip, and our product, could not possibly work in CES mode and they carefully and emphatically explained how this made no sense. Instead of digging into code, I looked at the chip's documentation and found the configuration table that changes the mode options for a T1/E1 channel.

Surprisingly the configuration table didn't have a CES setting, but it looked odd because there was an option for CAS. That stands for Channel Associated Signaling, the conveyance of old-fashioned analog signaling. Huh, maybe that was a single character spelling mistake? I called the chip vendor and asked this specific question, and the tech support engineer answered, "Of course that's a documentation error and it should be CES mode because CAS would make no sense in this context." Thank you.

I traveled to the office where the lead engineers worked and set up a meeting. What they didn't know was that in the lab next door to the meeting room, one of my team's engineers already had CES mode working and demonstrable. I asked the lead engineers again about CES mode support, and again they explained to me how this couldn't work. On cue, my engineer walked in from the lab next door, "the CES demo is ready!"

Grasping at Straws

Hank walks up to me, holding a 3.5" floppy diskette, says that it came from a customer, and it crashes any computer it's inserted into. I'm game. I took the disk, inserted it into my desktop computer, the disk drive whirred a moment, and the computer crashed.

When pursuing a bug in a production system when there is no clue as to the cause, it's important to begin with some theory about what could trigger the bug so you have somewhere to start a diagnostic process. In this case, I noticed that the diskette was labeled with Japanese writing, so I hypothesized that some multi-byte character was mistakenly interpreted as a control code that triggered some unusual code path. I could tell from Hank's reaction that he knew I was grasping at straws, but it's a start.

I asked him to get a serial cable and to set up a terminal, and meanwhile I would rebuild the filesystem to output every character in a filename to the serial port as the filenames were being scanned. I wanted to catch this rogue control character in the act. We got this set up, I inserted the diskette, the disk drive whirred a moment, and my computer crashed. We walked over to the terminal and saw a single character. A space.

In all of the billions of files read by many of the planet's largest enterprises using our operating system as well as our internal test regime, no one ever thought to start a filename with a space. Of course my control-code hypothesis was junk, but the diagnostic process quickly led us to find the real cause. The generalization of this scenario is actually quite common: a user generates some input that the system designers never imagined would happen, so there was never a test that could catch it.

No Straws to Grasp At

My team had recently built the first web-based enterprise email service. It was a new approach to give customers a product to run that would become their private web service on the Internet. There were very few bug reports from customers, but one customer in particular claimed that every few days their service would crash. No one else reported this, so it's tempting to dismiss the outlier, but this problem was too serious. Where to start?

We were running one of these services for our own engineering department, so I took a detailed look at the process health on our own server, and noticed that one thread seemed to be growing in memory. At that rate, I calculated that our server would crash in three days, and sure enough three days later it crashed, so at least now we would be chasing a memory leak if this was even the same problem, which there was no evidence to even assume that. And with our internal server rebooted, we had no way to reproduce or otherwise diagnose the problem.

With nothing else to go on, in utter exasperation, I printed out the web traffic log for the prior several days. It was a huge stack of tractor-feed paper showing the results of every user click, a morass of user-agent strings that describe the user's browser plus the protocol action they invoked. I started looking at every line, page after page with no idea what I was looking for. Just, maybe, an error report or something out of the ordinary. I'm getting bleary cross-eyed, line after line after line trudging through the log. Eventually I looked at one line, and exclaimed "Hank!" (yes, the same Hank).

I walked over to Hank and asked if he had been using our email service, and he said yes. Then I asked if he was still using OS/2 Warp instead of Windows, and he said yes of course. Then I rang up the account manager and asked if his troubled customer was an IBM shop, he said completely. Aha! Then I walked over to the lead developer, and said only, "It's Hank!" He stared for a few moments, frowned, shot a finger in the air, then jumped into the code and a few minutes later we had the fix. He knew Hank was an OS/2 fan.

There was nothing in our web-based product that would have been sensitive to different browsers, but that little stop button next to the address bar at the top of the browser initiates a particular protocol sequence. From a web server perspective, it's okay for a browser to crash, but the stop button is special. It turns out that the Netscape browser running on OS/2 Warp violated the stop button protocol because of a bug, leaving the server hanging on a response from the browser that never happened, leaking some memory every time. It's an easy enough fix, and an important reminder that network transmissions can fail at *any* time, and often the most inconvenient of times.

Recap

It is important to think about software quality inclusive of user interfaces, because that is how most users experience the systems they interact with and often what drives frustration and a sense of poor quality. Not every user interface should prioritize aesthetics, nor sacrifice user satisfaction in the name of achieving a particular aesthetic. Taking an experimental approach can yield significant improvements in user experience, especially when the experiments can be conducted as live variations in the market.

Complex real-time systems will encounter situations that their designers could not have specifically defined nor tested for, yet they will be perceived to have faulty quality when they perform poorly and result in unfortunate outcomes. Then there are some real-time systems that are designed for situations that may only happen extremely rarely, which raises the questions of whether such systems can be adequately tested and trusted. These are increasingly implemented using Artificial Intelligence, which should cause us to think about system testing and quality in broader terms than we do today.

When systems are more deterministic and testable, debugging is an essential tool. The trickiest problems are often better solved with reasoning and following clues than diving deep into a debugging tool, because this can reveal the mechanism that caused the bug. Even if a bug isn't a result of a coding error, for example if it is caused by an electronics bug or documentation error, it will still be the responsibility of a software engineer to figure out how to compensate and put a correction into production.

CHAPTER 10

Business Principles

If you are managing a software project, you are managing money and running a business.

I see your eyes glazing over with this talk about money and business. But that is exactly the point! Too many Engineering Managers and even Product Managers think that someone else is taking care of these things, and that is not good for business. You need to be engaged.

You may think that your purpose is to build software, but that is just a means to the important reason that you are employed: to make money. Your software could be making money as a product that is sellable, or services that customers will pay for, or productivity improvements to lower costs or accelerate other work efforts, but in the end it all needs to generate financial gains, else it will stop. This is true even for non-profit organizations, contracting work, and enterprise applications although sometimes the revenue, or positive benefit, may be more abstract and harder to measure.

In this chapter, we will take a look at software development from a money perspective, which will help us to make strategic pivots over the lifecycle of a product, and to build out frameworks for making investment decisions regarding which software projects are preferable because they will produce better returns. It doesn't really matter what your product is or what market you're in, the shape of these fundamentals will mostly hold true. The following discusses software finances from the perspective of a mostly software product being built and introduced into the market

© David J. Asher 2024
D. J. Asher, *Mastering the Complex World of Software Management,*
https://doi.org/10.1007/979-8-8688-0841-8_10

for sale, so it's a generalized view that may need some tweaking for your own situation. Much of this applies to other kinds of products, although so many electronic products have such a high level of software content that this treatment is applicable to many situations.

Expenses

Expenses are the monies that get spent in building and operating your software. How can you know the actual expenses related to your software project? You may have an explicit budget that you control, but a budget only represents approved plans and not actual spending. There is probably someone in the finance department of your company that tracks this information or can generate it, and is assigned to your area. Seek them out and make friends; they are tired of being ignored and will usually be happy to hear someone take an active interest.

We will partition the expense curve over the product lifecycle into three phases: Investment, Maintenance, and Decline, as in Figure 10-1.

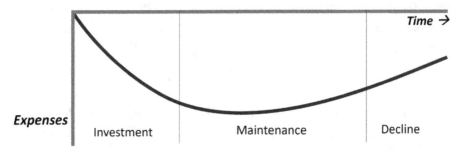

Figure 10-1. *Expense curve*

Investment is the first phase, where expenses incurred during product development are investments because investors are hoping to gain future revenues far exceeding their outlays, and just like a purchase of some company's stock, there is significant risk that your endeavor won't succeed to profitability. During this phase your financial position is all cost and you aren't yet able to sustain your own team with revenues and the good output of your work. It is important to respect that other people are putting their money and confidence into your ability to turn a concept into a sellable product or other productive function, in a reasonable amount of time, with limited resources, and excellent quality. Software development is human capital-intensive and people are investing in you.

Maintenance is when your software is offered to the market or is otherwise being used by its intended consumers, at scale. Almost all software launches with a limited set of features and a considerable backlog of features desired but cut from its introduction. This backlog grows as customers understand the limitations of your software and demand more. Sometime during this phase, a company will make a choice about continuing to expand the software team in order to generate even more growth, or stabilize or even curtail team size in order to put money into other areas promising to be more profitable. You may feel dejected if your company makes a decision to downsize your team; it isn't personal, it's just business.

Decline is the phase that we don't like to think about, but eventually all technologies surrender to something newer. Even if your software is a great hit with customers, it will eventually need to be replaced and the revenues will slow or stop. When there is no longer growth in your product, but there are active customers that will continue to pay for it, a company will typically look for ways to lower the project's expenses, both headcount and operations. Headcount is usually the easiest expense to control, and a company may decide to simply lower the headcount and force efficiency on the team, or find an offshore team or contractor that is lower cost, or just shut it down.

Revenues

Revenues are the money that comes in from selling your software or otherwise exploiting your software to get others to pay you such as advertisements. Now let's look at the revenue trend over time, where the four phases of the revenue cycle are Introduction, Growth, Competition, and Stagnation, as in Figure 10-2.

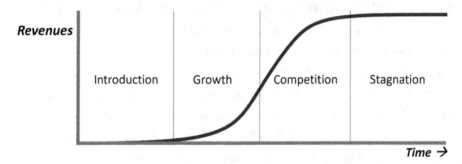

Figure 10-2. *Revenue curve*

The *Introduction* phase is not very useful in the market in terms of generating revenue because there isn't a product yet, except that a powerful product launch could set up for faster results later on. One of those techniques is a beta test or other form of limited product introduction that builds awareness and demand, and may help to refine your product just before launch. Even if an early introduction generates some revenue, it is inconsequential for your project's finances. But in any case, by the end of the Introduction phase, you have customers and some business model that promises to generate revenue.

The *Growth* phase is where customers are enjoying your product and every day sees more customers added and revenues increasing. Companies almost always and proudly describe revenue growth as exponential, a percentage increase such as month-to-month or year-over-year. This approach is intuitive because you can take the ratio of last month's revenues into this month's revenues and come up with a growth factor represented as a percentage increase. When this goes on for a few years, a company may even derive its compound annual growth rate (CAGR), reinforcing the idea that your business is enjoying exponential growth. However, as a model of what is actually happening to your revenues, it is not correct! We will come back to this discussion in a moment.

The *Competition* phase puts sales pressure on your product because you were successful and others want a piece of that money pie. When they get their piece, your growth will slow down unless you somehow make the total pie bigger, and you now have a strategic change to make if you want to keep the revenue flowing against the headwinds of competition. At some point your sales growth will slow because you have simply saturated the market and there are few new customers to be acquired.

It is important to note a special case of competition – monopoly. Whether due to its strategic brilliance or maniacal aggressiveness or illegal practices or damned good luck, a monopoly has suppressed or intimidated or swallowed all significant competition and the pie is mostly theirs. In terms of our revenue model, it really doesn't make a difference. Even monopolies will saturate their target market at some point and find it nearly impossible to acquire new customers, and then their growth phase will also come to an end.

Then it's *Stagnation* once the Competition phase has played out. If your software is in this phase, your approach and strategy need to change again, to figure out how to eke out the most revenue while conserving all costs. At some point, even Stagnation may run its course and then you have some unhappy exit decisions to make.

Growth Model

Let's consider the model we typically use to describe growth expressed as a percentage change over a period. Does this rate of growth continue forever? Of course, you know that it doesn't. Given the Competition and Stagnation phases, this model is only a short-term approximation to what really happens to revenues, and only applies to the Growth phase. All products encounter slowing growth at some point.

A more accurate model than exponential growth would be an s-curve, also known as a sigmoid function, which is a class of curves that have the similar property of starting at zero, growing through an inflection point, then stabilizing to some value – just like our revenue curve above. The inflection point is where you can see that growth stops increasing and starts to slow down. A common and simple example is the logistic function, $f(t) = 1/(1+e^{-t})$. You could parameterize the numerator for scale and the time variable to have the model conform to your situation, as in: $f(t) = A/(1+e^{-Bt})$.

Now, I'm not a pedantic dreamer (or whatever the mathematical equivalent of a pedant is) expecting the world to start adopting A and B parameters to describe their growth patterns. That would just feel too weird and complicated for most people, compared to the simple and familiar percentage growth model that we like to use. However, you should understand the impact of using the wrong model on your thoughts and actions. When in one month growth is reported at a particular level, say 18%, then if the next month it is lower, say 12%, alarms will go off. This change doesn't mean that your project is suddenly operating at a loss, or even that it stopped growing, it is just saying that the rate of growth is slowing.

There could be many factors that are driving the change, such as seasonality or fluctuations in the economy. If you can explain these factors, then you may be comfortable not to react urgently when your growth rate dips a bit. But if this change continues or gets worse, or if you can see that a competitor has made a change in the market situation that is impacting your revenue, then this change in growth rate could be a warning sign that action is needed.

Here's where using the wrong model can cause distortion: if the managers and leaders of your product believe that there should be continued growth and see the slowing increase in revenues as an emergency to get back to continued growth. This change may in fact be a signal of reaching the growth inflection point, in which case it is informing you that market saturation is approaching, and you may need to change your marketing mode from new customer acquisition to generating more revenue per existing customer.

Net Income

What a company really wants to know is, how much money are we earning? At a corporate level, this would be called profit. At your program level, it is sometimes called contribution, as in the extent that your product contributes to overall profitability. Here we'll use the term *net income*, and it is simply the difference between revenues and expenses. This is crucial to know because when it is positive and therefore producing a gain (i.e., operating in the black), then there is growth and bonuses and free lunch and everyone is so happy. And when it is negative and producing a loss (i.e., operating in the red), your perks and budgets are cut and then you are at risk of losing your job because you are going out of business. The history of the color code is that accountants use red ink to show losses and black ink to show profits.

Over the lifecycle of a product (Figure 10-3), you want net income to be in the black but you always start in the red.

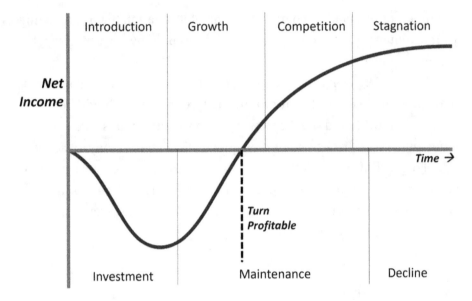

Figure 10-3. *Net income curve*

Just as revenues and expenses follow a typical curve throughout the lifecycle of a software product, so does net income. When you are operating in the Investment phase and the product hasn't been introduced yet, everything you do is a financial loss. The fact that you enter the market and start selling your product doesn't pull you out of a loss, you have to be far enough along the Growth phase that revenues exceed expenses. When you delay the introduction of your product, you keep paying the expenses but deprive yourself of revenues, therefore your net income stays negative and you keep operating at a loss.

While the shape of the net income curve over the lifecycle of a product may be hard to escape, there is nothing preordained that demands it ever go positive. Some companies can experience customer and revenue growth for a long time, but if their business model doesn't push revenues significantly higher than expenses, they will be operating at a loss even at massive scale. Some companies can sustain having individual products operating at lower gains or even a loss over long periods if they have other products that realize gains, or maybe they have investors that keep pouring money in, but those magical sources of money always seem to stop at some point, so you may want to focus on your business model from the start.

If your business model is robust, then once you get to a point where revenues far exceed expenses and the customer base is still growing, it will be like printing money. This is where a software-based business can show spectacular returns on investment, but it takes careful focus to build such a successful business model.

Profitability and Breakeven

Knowing how net income behaves over a product lifecycle, we can take this one step further and look at accumulated net income, referred to as retained earnings at the corporate reporting level, which would be the sum of all gains and losses since the start of the program (Figure 10-4). Before a product becomes profitable, the accumulated net income curve keeps getting more and more negative, and doesn't bottom-out until the moment that net income crosses from loss to gain, or we could say the moment when the business turns profitable.

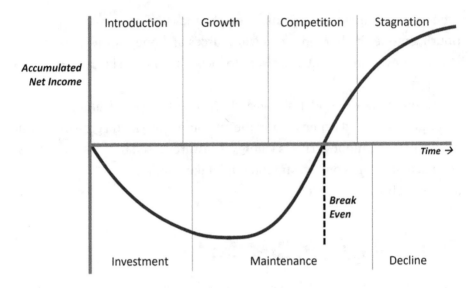

Figure 10-4. *Accumulated net income curve*

From an investor standpoint, their investment has not produced any return before profitability happens, and even after turning profitable, would still be a loss for investors for quite some time. It is only after enough profits have been made to the extent where the accumulated net income reaches zero and the business has reached the break-even point. This is effectively the earliest that an investment has at least been earned back, and it is only significantly after the break-even point that a business has sufficient accumulated net income that we can consider there to be a possibility of return on investment.

Strategic Pivots

Transitions between the Introduction, Growth, Competition, and Stagnation revenue phases require changes in product strategy. Cooperation between Product Managers and Engineering Managers is essential to be able to react to changes in market conditions and ensure that your product remains profitable. As a manager with great responsibility over the expense side of your project's finances, and being a concerned actor in the revenues side, you have a few strategic goals through these transitions:

1. Introduce the product into the market as early as is reasonable to enable a transition from Investment to Growth, and to make it harder for competitors to enter. If there is no competition when you introduce your product, you gain a first mover advantage. But if you are following others, you need to present compelling features to lure customers.

2. Extend the sales growth inflection point for as long as possible by continually introducing features that keep you ahead of the competition.

3. Shift from a focus on new customer acquisition to harvesting more revenue per customer once the market is showing signs of saturation and slowing growth.

4. Manage costs carefully in the Maintenance and Decline phases, being sensitive to the situation where product enhancements may not result in higher revenues.

For all of these things, you have to know where you are in the product lifecycle in order to make these decisions correctly and with the right timing. Changes in net income trends over time can be a strong signal that helps indicate when strategic pivots are necessary.

The Asset Cycle

Here's what product development companies do: convert expenses to assets that generate revenues, where the money to pay those expenses come from revenues or from loans or from investments. In this undertaking, the company will accrue liabilities which are obligations that are expected to reduce the future value of total assets. The net difference between assets and liabilities is equity, often expressed as shareholder value.

In the case of software companies, when we write code we are converting expenses to assets. The primary expense is compensation for the coders and others involved, with most other expenses grouped as operations.

It is not unusual to find it difficult to determine the accurate value of an asset. Stocks are a great example, where the value is realized only when a stock is sold, which makes stock valuations subject to variable and unpredictable market conditions. That inability to accurately know the value of an asset does not preclude us from making a reasonable estimate of its value. Those estimates may be easier to make when there's a market for the asset such as publicly traded stocks, and would be based on assumptions or conventions when the market is limited or the assets are privately held.

Your software is an asset. Writing code will generate assets although the monetary value of those assets could be questionable or unrealized; that's a business problem to figure out how to deploy code to achieve financial benefits from software assets. Unfortunately it is all too easy to expend resources writing software that is unproductive as an asset.

Software Asset Value

If software is an asset, is it like a diamond? Can you take several well-known characteristics and assign a value based on those characteristics and present market conditions? That's not a bad conceptual model, but the details for understanding a software asset are far more subtle and complex. In the following, let's define software broadly, to include all source and executing code, data captured in databases, algorithms, any intellectual property encoded in the software, and all of the process and operations to build it and make it work.

The whole purpose of writing software is to execute some functionality, so let's start with the first asset being the functionality that was intended and assume that you and your team are good coders that deliver on your commitments. The activity of writing any piece of code may further accrue any of the asset characteristics described in the following. Unlike a diamond, you can't simply look up their value in a chart, and there won't be an open market to use as a value baseline, but knowing the range of characteristics can give you a framework for evaluating software asset value.

Connection to Revenue: If your software is generating revenue, that could represent a hard correlation to asset value; however, there are probably other factors contributing to a positive financial asset value, such as trademarks and marketing efforts.

Potential to Generate Revenue: If software is not currently deployed toward generating revenue, it still may have the potential to do so at a future date, or possibly it could be used in a different way than originally intended and thereby expand its revenue potential.

Potential to Be Sold: Software assets can be licensed or sold to other entities as another stream of revenue; however, you should also consider that this could impinge on your own ability to generate revenue.

Competitive Advantage: If you are competing against similar products or services and the quality and functionality of your software proves to be superior, that could enable faster revenue generation, or the ability to introduce market-leading features at a faster pace.

Reputational and Brand Advantage: Would you rather be known in the marketplace as a company that makes software that is delightful to use, or that frustrates its users? Great software is a brand asset.

Customer Satisfaction: Levels of customer satisfaction can be measured in ways other than revenue that also increase the value of software assets, such as low support burden, high customer ratings, or impressive Net Promoter Score.

Intellectual Property: Much of the volume of written software is fairly low in marketable IP value, but some software assets may hold critical trade secrets, or even implement patented innovations.

Lowering Costs: From a profitability perspective of a large organization, it can be as valuable for a software asset to lower costs as it is to generate revenue.

Productivity Improvement: A special case of cost reduction is improving the productivity of developers or other functions in a company. Saving time is like saving money when one of the largest expenses is salary, or gives you a speed advantage in the market.

Architectural Foundation: Some software serve as infrastructure for other layers of software. Its asset value increases when new layers can be developed faster, at higher quality, or with lower skilled workers.

Instructional Insight: Some code serves as a precedent for future coders, because of clean and effective style or approach. In a large code base, coders usually know where the good code is and who wrote it.

Open Source Community: If it applies to your situation, ownership or contributions into an open source program can lead to industry connections, finding talent, accelerating innovation, and other rewards.

Social Good: Some companies maintain a second bottom line to reflect the social good they promote in the world. Think about how the software you create can also serve these non-financial missions.

Software Liabilities

Generating asset value from software is speculative; generating liabilities is assured. The set of liabilities builds with every line of code written, we just tend to ignore them until something boils over to a crisis. Some of these manifest as explicit costs, or may be a drag on productivity, while others can be viewed as business risks that should be considered. Just like a financial liability, a software liability can reduce your equity by putting downward pressure on the value of your software assets.

Bugs: If you write code, you're writing bugs. If bugs escape the development process and get caught by the quality team, it slows development and adds cost by spending time on efforts that aren't generating new features. If bugs escape into production and impact the customer experience, damage to reputation can cause revenue to decline.

Technical Debt: Larger systems of code will suffer increasing maintenance costs over time, as some components are made obsolete by newer approaches or technologies, become vulnerable to security hacks, have dependencies that may become deprecated, or may have proven to be built in a way that makes it too hard to work with. The choices for remediation are to eliminate, replace, work around, or rewrite the offending code – all expensive and disruptive undertakings that don't increase asset value, just prevent it from deteriorating.

Dependency Surprises: So much software these days incorporates third party open-source packages or online services, and those also have their own dependencies, forming a supply chain that may be very hard to know accurately. Once in a while, something breaks in one of those dependencies, and your choices are to upgrade the component, find a work-around, find a replacement, or change your approach.

Security Vulnerabilities: You've done nothing, but someone else pokes your software and finds a way to exploit it, compromising the integrity of your product and endangering your customers. If you're very lucky, it's your own security team that found it, less lucky if it's a security researcher, and out of luck when it's a hacker. Most often you will have no choice except to immediately put resources on fixing the vulnerability, accepting the work disruption.

Data Loss or Leakage: A software vulnerability may result in the loss or leakage of proprietary or customer data. This could be the corruption or deletion of data that customers entrusted you to hold, or unintentional or malicious leakage of private data to untrusted parties. Ultimately, it was a weakness in your software that enabled a data loss or leak to happen. That weakness is probably repairable and becomes an urgent and disruptive task; however, the data loss or leak itself, and any knock-on business consequences, may not be so easy to fix. Your code has a higher liability if it is less robust against these threats.

Competitive Disadvantage: When two companies are competing, the market may find one of them to have built superior software, which leaves the other at a competitive disadvantage no matter how clever the engineers thought their code is. What do you do with code that is losing in the market? Its liability increases.

Customer Dissatisfaction: The flip side of customer satisfaction is when your code makes customers unhappy. In many cases, the extent of dissatisfaction is measurable and it is better to get that data than to remain in the dark about it. Customer dissatisfaction could be a harbinger of business decline if left to fester.

Instructional Spoilage: Just as great code can set a positive example that instructs many others to write better code, some code can set an example that leads to layering of disadvantageous practices – we often call these antipatterns.

License or IP infringement: The trolls really are out there. Your team may use some open source program without fully understanding the implications of its license, or infringe on a foundational copyright or utility patent. This scenario doesn't necessarily end in legal nightmares and high costs if your code can be brought into compliance, but that fix could be a disruptive and costly process that wasn't planned. Or it could blow up.

Software Balance Sheet

When companies need to publish their equity, it is expressed as a set of assets and liabilities on a balance sheet. It is balanced because equity = assets - liabilities, always. Since we just discussed frameworks for you to establish the asset and liability values of your software, you have the opportunity to create a software balance sheet. You wouldn't want to apply a balance sheet analysis to every small project, but never coming to understand your software balance sheet may put you in a position that weighs heavily on liabilities and you won't even know it. You may think that your software liability value cannot exceed its asset value, but just like a corporate balance sheet this is quite possible and a terribly risky position to be in.

You can also predict assets and liabilities for software that you are considering for investment, i.e., future expenses that convert to assets and liabilities. You can use your software balance sheet to determine which project is more likely to build stronger assets and lower liabilities. You would then have a framework for making evidence-based business decisions about software investment, and the ability to look beyond the technical happy path. We tend to become risk-averse when making investment decisions because, although the future asset values are seductive, the liability values may be overwhelming.

The Myth of Sunk Costs

During product planning sessions, it's inevitable: when considering which programs get investment, which get life support, and which get reduced or eliminated, engineers and managers will cite the principle of *Sunk Costs*. They interpret this to mean that once money has already been spent, you don't get a mulligan to spend that money again, so don't consider the work you've already done, just look forward. Money spent is water under the bridge.

This interpretation considers software development to be ephemeral, like throwing a party, having no productive outcome. So if your past investment decision didn't have the full outcome that you were expecting, move on. This is a wrong interpretation and it is damaging to understand software in this way because you didn't simply spend that money, you converted it to a software asset.

Software development is an act of converting an expense (developer salaries) into an asset (the code that was written). To understand the distinction, follow the money. In the case of a party, buying food and entertainment and such, cash outflows to outsiders. In the case of software development, cash goes to your own developers that write code to increase your own wealth of intellectual property. You have converted spent money into your own asset.

When making investment decisions, you need to consider how you might possibly exploit the assets that you have, not the money you've spent. Thinking about software as a sunk cost without considering its asset value denies you a rational way to make investment decisions and fully capitalize on the investments already made. You can't play a long game with sunk cost thinking.

Low-Risk Investments

The lowest risk software investments are maintenance activities like bug fixes and security patching. It is quite easy to justify the need, and all of the issues are probably well-documented bug reports and security incidents. The risks are low since you know your own code and will only make small changes to apply a fix. Value is being maintained with each action completed because factors that degrade value are being eliminated, though it is hard to argue that any value is being created with maintenance activities.

Most ongoing software programs have a backlog of work such as productivity improvements, automation of operations, code refactoring, and similar enhancements generally viewed as maintenance. These are also low risk since the internal cost factors are fairly well understood and it should be easy to demonstrate the incremental value of improvement, even if that value does not directly translate to increasing customer adoption or revenues.

Incremental feature changes that are directly demanded by customers is another low risk category. You don't need to be concerned with customer acceptance since customers asked for the feature, so you are eliminating the risk factor of not knowing whether any customers will enjoy the new feature and keep using your product.

Longstanding programs tend to build up a considerable backlog of such maintenance tasks so there is no shortage of ideas. But of course there is a very good reason why many of these backlog tasks don't get done: resource constraints. No engineering manager gets all of the resources that would be required to achieve all desired feature development, maintenance tasks, explorations, and bold initiatives. The very act of prioritizing one task for development means that some others will not get done, and that is known as opportunity cost.

Opportunity cost is what keeps us from completing all known software maintenance. At some point, a software program will accumulate such a backlog of maintenance tasks that it would seem little else could get done, and that is an undesirable outcome for revenues, customer satisfaction, employee retention, and growth. But if too much of the maintenance backlog is ignored, the quality of the software product will degrade to such an extent that it will threaten revenues, customer satisfaction, employee retention, and growth. What a pickle.

What's the right amount of investment in software maintenance? Risk aversion, meaning that we seek to make decisions that are low risk because we fear the consequences of high-risk decisions, can drive us overwhelmingly to the safety of maintenance investments to the detriment of our competitive advantage. Successful programs figure out the level of maintenance investment that becomes "just good enough" and not any more.

If not maintenance, how about internal recommendations for improvements? Surely the developers know the product inside and out, and have a good sense of what is needed, no? It turns out, not so much. Developers tend to be focused on specific technical aspects and often can't see a product as a whole, much less how it is used by customers and perceived in the market against competition. So engineering recommendations to improve their own code and operations may have real value but skepticism is required and again, investing too much in this category is an opportunity cost at odds with growth.

Incremental feature changes, as defined by Product Managers, would hold great promise as low-risk investments because they have already been validated with customers. That may be true, but there may also be a gap between validation with a few customers, and acceptance from the market. This is a common trap, especially for upstart companies that are anxious to please any customer, because that incremental feature may only delight a small number of customers, and carries an opportunity cost of not developing a growth feature that appeals more broadly to the market.

High-Risk Investments

The highest risk investments are innovative features, or new products or services without a track record in the market. A decision to proceed is based on some market insight, which may or may not have an evidence basis. For example, a product that reduces cost or eliminates pain for enterprise IT users often stands a good chance of success and the market opportunity may even be measurable. The opposite end of having an evidence basis is introducing a novel consumer product in a category that doesn't exist, expecting that buyers will want it but they don't know it yet.

Let's presume for a moment that we have perfect knowledge that a new product will be a hit in the market, so customer adoption and market acceptance risks are minimal. There would still be significant execution risk getting to market. There are so many vulnerabilities:

- What if the project team fails to deliver the needed functionality?

- What if poor software quality creates more problems than benefits?

- What if a critical developer leaves in the middle of the project?

- What if the project takes too long to develop and the company relinquishes a market opportunity to a competitor?

- What if software delivery is executed perfectly but marketing or pricing or sales missteps cause it to fail in the market?

When the market upside is huge, so are the risks. It's important to try and identify any risk exposure before making an investment decision, and re-evaluate risks at a checkpoint during development. For one thing, it is possible that an identified risk is so outstanding that it strongly militates against the investment. For another, knowing and honestly facing the risk, the project team may be able to address it head-on and improve their odds of success.

Acquisitions As De-risking Development

I've seen many engineers shaking their heads after the announcement of an acquisition – *we could have built that, and for way less money!* Well, maybe. But consider the above list of project execution risks, and it should become clear that the high premium paid for an acquisition is assigning a value against a large set of risks that the company would otherwise be facing with an internal development project.

A successful startup has essentially de-risked all of the execution challenges, and deserves a price premium. In the cases of the most valuable startup acquisitions, they have built a customer base and thereby de-risked the greatest unknown in new product introductions – market acceptance.

There is one other cost that is important to consider: the time value of not being present in the market while a product is being developed. Falling behind competitors and forgoing revenue for lack of a product to sell are very steep penalties that can be solved with an acquisition.

Wow, all of that good stuff is coming with an acquisition! Of course, there are risks, too. Such as: Is the product what it claims to be and with advertised quality? Do the development and other teams have a conflicting culture? How costly and disruptive will the integration of the startup be? Are there landmines like contract defaults, infringement cases, or financial shenanigans? At least if you acquire, do it eyes wide open.

Recap

A software program, like any business, is dynamic over its lifecycle but follows a familiar pattern. Expenses are incurred from the very start of a program, but revenues will only be generated once customers or other money sources, such as advertisers, are paying you. Expenses can be partitioned over three phases across a product lifecycle: Investment, Maintenance, and Decline. Revenues can be partitioned over four phases: Introduction, Growth, Competition, and Stagnation. We often represent revenue growth as a percentage increase over a prior time period but that is misleading; the more accurate model is an s-curve that does not lead anyone to believe that growth will continue indefinitely.

The difference between revenue and expense is net income, which expresses profitability. When software programs reach profitability and then scale massively, they have the potential to generate enormous profits over time. From an investor standpoint, it can take a long time before enough profits have accumulated to compensate for prior losses, known as the break-even point. Even then, it can take much longer to realize a return on investment. Knowing how growth and profitability change over the lifecycle of a software product enables its leaders to make strategic pivot decisions that can preserve profitability.

When a team writes code, it is converting investments into software assets, and it is those assets that are exploited to generate revenue. It is speculative whether software assets will ever result in a profitable business, but it is guaranteed that writing code produces liabilities. We can look deeply at many factors influencing software asset value and liabilities to realize a software balance sheet, which can be a tool to help us understand the equity value of our software and how to make better informed decisions about software investments. We should not use a model of sunk costs when making software investment decisions because investments in coding do not disappear, rather they are converted to assets.

Once a software program has survived for several years, it will usually accrue a backlog of maintenance tasks and minor feature requests. These can be low risk investments, but focussing too much on maintenance activities will carry an opportunity cost of precluding higher growth and profits because high-risk and high-return projects aren't being worked on. Acquisitions are often an attractive approach to achieving high returns because many of the execution risks and market acceptance risks have already been resolved.

CHAPTER 11

Driving Innovation

Innovation is not something that happens to you; it is something that you *do*. If you claim to have an innovative team but passively wait for innovation to happen, you will be disappointed. No matter how you may judge a team's creativity and intelligence, if they are actively engaged in acts of innovation they will be far more likely to succeed at it. Nor is technology innovation accomplished with a one-and-done brainstorming session, rather it yields to those who persevere. The best part is that an innovation process can be learned and managed, but you should expect the best results if it is a sustained endeavor and permeates your culture.

A Primer on Intellectual Property (IP)

It has only been since 1994 when a US court ruling clarified that an invention based on software can be patented. As a result of this history, much of the software industry evolved under conditions that presumed patents could not be obtained for software, leaving most software developers disinterested and unaware of the basics of intellectual property. Let's address that, and start with the foundations of IP and how they relate to software.

A **trademark** is some recognizable text or image that is associated with a particular organization, service, or product, distinguishing it from all others. This is one area of IP where it doesn't matter if the product

© David J. Asher 2024
D. J. Asher, *Mastering the Complex World of Software Management,*
https://doi.org/10.1007/979-8-8688-0841-8_11

is software. The trademark itself can command a huge value when its product has become successful – you know you've hit the top when your product's trademarked name becomes a verb.

A *copyright* is a particular expression of a creative work, so for software it refers to the actual source code that you've written, the machine code compiled from your source code, or other unique aspects of your software such as an API definition. Copyrights do not protect the ideas behind a creative work such as algorithms, only the manner and likeness in which those ideas are expressed. Even if this makes perfect sense to you, there is much room for interpretation.

A *design patent* protects the way something looks, so generally would not be applicable to code, except that design patents can be used to protect visual elements of software such as user interface icon designs.

A *utility patent* protects the way something works, but not just any old thing; it must be an *invention*. To qualify for a patent, your invention must be *novel* and *nonobvious* when compared to the *prior art*, and you must be able to adequately describe its operation in a *patent application* such that someone *skilled in the art* can reproduce it. All of these terms are precisely defined by patent office documentation and laws, but put together mean that you are introducing a useful idea that the world has never seen before in quite the way that you are doing it. Once a patent is granted, it is published so anyone can see your invention, increasing the world's knowledge. In exchange for your great gift of exposing the inner workings of your invention to humanity, a patent grants you a market monopoly for a limited period of time.

A *trade secret* is quite the opposite of a patent because only a privileged few people are allowed access to some knowledge, which could cover almost anything from your source code to a manufacturing process to a recipe. The rest of us don't know what's in your trade secret because … it's a secret. And if you truly care for your trade secret, then you have legal recourse if you find that someone has stolen and misused it, because that would be theft.

Infringement is when another party abuses the intellectual property rights granted to them. For example, everyone is granted the right to read your patent and understand your invention, and even use that knowledge to circumvent your monopoly by creating a different invention. Once someone abuses that knowledge and takes actions that are beyond their granted rights, such as manufacturing your invention without your permission, then they are infringing your IP rights. For a party to legally obtain rights to your IP, you can write a license that grants specific permissions. Such an IP license is just a special kind of contract.

It is common to use the term *protection* when discussing intellectual property, which refers to protection from others that seek to infringe your IP rights. This idea of protection might conjure up visions of Big Government looking out for infringers of your IP and bringing them to justice, righting the wrong of abusing your IP. Unfortunately, that is never the case. Governments don't have such kinds of surveillance, nor have any inclination to spend their time identifying and chasing infringers on your behalf. Protection means that you have the ability to identify infringers and bring them to legal action, such as a lawsuit. Sometimes just the threat of a lawsuit is sufficient to get an infringer to agree to a settlement or arbitration, because an IP lawsuit is costly and messy for all parties involved.

If you are innovating, then you are generating *confidential information.* Most engineering aspects of product development would broadly be described as confidential information. As an engineer or a manager for a company, you have an obligation to handle confidential information carefully and never distribute it to unauthorized parties. Your company should have policies governing confidential information, and you may have signed an employment agreement that details your obligations. The most important thing to know is that confidential information doesn't get shared with people outside of your company except under the control of a *Non-Disclosure Agreement* (NDA), which again, your company has policies and forms to handle these.

Technology companies often have an IP office with lawyers that can assist in getting inventions through the patent process. As a Software Manager you may not believe that your work has IP value, but discussion with your tech leads and an IP lawyer may convince you otherwise, especially if you are creating competitive advantages for your company.

A Primer on Open Source

An *open source license* is similar to a patent in that it allows for publication of your creative work for the world to see and make improvements, but rather than a monopoly granted through a patent application, the use of your creative work is governed by the terms of its license. The purpose of an open source license is to grant those rights without cost, but to also impose some restrictions to prevent misuse of your software – and it's up to the license writer to figure out what "misuse" means.

If your goal is to make money from your software, why would you give it away? This question has bothered many people for a long time, but the effectiveness of open source software (OSS) has proven itself so many times over that it has become fully accepted as a rational business model. Most large open source programs have corporate backers or foundations that fund software development, maintenance, and to some extent, marketing. Multiple companies, even competitors, make contributions to the same program because they have a common business interest in that software thriving.

Smaller programs may have different motivations to publish as open source because they aren't as likely to attract contributors. Individuals may publish small programs as a way of enhancing their reputation and building their network. Companies may publish small programs when they are adjuncts to their primary software and not so financially important on their own.

A company that is the license holder of OSS may use it to generate income by packaging and distributing it with other software, extending it with proprietary functionality, or providing specialized services. More than a few OSS programs simply started with the business model of generating a large following and intending to be acquired, not worrying too much about revenue generation and profitability.

A *permissive* open source license puts minimal restrictions on the use of its code and allows for derivative works to be proprietary. A *copyleft* open source license allows for broad use and sharing; however, derivative works retain the exact same open source license and the terms of the license carry forward to future derivative works. Within these two broad categories, there are several well established license models: GNU General Public License (GPL); GNU Lesser General Public License (LGPL); Apache 2.0 License; Berkeley Software Distribution (BSD); Common Development and Distribution License (CDDL); Eclipse Public License (EPL); Microsoft Public License (MS-PL); and MIT License. Each of these license types has particular properties, and some are even short and easy to understand.

While you can write your own open source license, doing so would invite trouble because it takes lawyers extra time to evaluate something unknown, and poses extra risk of using software governed by an unfamiliar license. Most OSS will simply use an established license with little or no modification.

Working with Open Source Software

There are several ways to be involved with open source software, and it is important to understand the implications of the license for any of these.

Using OSS: In most cases, using OSS does not incur payment to the license holder or even a requirement to get permission. This even holds true for commercial purposes, for example if you use an OSS program for internal data processing of customer information. The most common example is the Linux operating system which is used widely and freely.

Distributing OSS: Distribution means that you literally transfer some open source software to a user, typically in compiled binary form, which could happen if you incorporate the OSS code into a product that is sold. For example, if you are producing lighting controllers that use Linux, then you may be able to use the software at no cost, but the license may impose very particular requirements about informing the user, so read the license carefully.

Owning OSS: If you are producing software and considering publishing it as open source, you should understand your license options and the business rationale for doing so. Once source code is published, there isn't a way to undo that decision. If a company has some trade secret software that is highly valuable such as an algorithm, they may publish the rest of their software as open source but retain the most sensitive parts as proprietary code.

Contributing to OSS: When a company strategically decides to be a contributor to an OSS program, they may make assignments for certain engineers to spend their time coding for it. Less formally, some engineers may need to contribute fixes or minor functionality just to make some OSS program work for their project. In some cases, engineers may work on OSS programs independently from their company's interests, and they should check your company's policies regulating independent coding activities before jumping in.

How to Invent

Invention is a response to a technical challenge. Many problems have fairly straightforward solutions using well-known approaches, which is really what the discipline of engineering is all about. But some problems are genuinely hard, where the more obvious solutions leave unacceptable drawbacks, and you may need to overcome these drawbacks in order to fulfill a product vision or establish a competitive advantage. An invention is a clever way to get past the bad parts, and maybe even introduce some surprising new good parts.

So let's say that you find yourself in this situation, what do you do, hire an inventor? If you are expecting that an invention emerges from a sudden spark of insight, that is in the realm of possibility, but only after a deep immersion into the problem space, even for an inventor. Often it isn't the spark that reveals an inventor, but their tenacity in wrestling a problem until it yields. Even so, a strategy that relies on a single person to perform this function reliably and on demand is a fragile one, even if such a person could be found and hired onto your team.

To tease innovation when it is needed, the more effective approach is to assemble an inventing team, which is not, per se, a team of inventors. It is a team of engineers that are willing to explore a problem deeply and exchange ideas without giving up. They should be dispatched with a clear description of the problem, a set of constraints, and some sense of what winning looks like. This group could be the team that you manage, or you might gather a cross-functional team spanning multiple disciplines to get a diverse set of perspectives. You don't need genius, but it would help if you could identify a few engineers that show out-of-the-box thinking. A wacky idea may not be directly useful, but it could dislodge entrenched thinking patterns and enable the group to see problems in a different way. Breakthroughs depend on the conditions that can reveal a solution hiding behind the mental barriers that we erect to prevent us from getting distracted by the unfamiliar.

If you are going to play the role of facilitator to the inventing team, you need to be careful not to offer your own solutions or show a particular bias. If the outcome turns out to be an invention, then the result should be surprising, which means it is not what you were thinking at the outset. The problem should also be stated as close to the intended use-case as you can get it, without getting too technical except to explain how current solutions are inadequate. A constraint may be the only factor that is relevant to the need for an invention, for example if you require a product to be offered at one-quarter of current pricing, or to perform better using half of the energy. A set of constraints will place bounds on the problem space and also challenge conventional thinking.

Progress will be made in fits and starts. You can't lock people into a conference room for two hours or even two days and expect that a hard problem will be solved, but pieces of the puzzle may emerge from a series of sessions. Some sessions will need to be longer than an hour, because it takes that long just for people to release themselves from their routine tasks and focus deeply on the problem. Your duty as a manager is to keep the exploration going, assign investigation tasks along the way, poke the team with challenging questions, pose scenarios that push the boundaries of the problem, and help the team to judge their results.

I learned this process of invention-through-perseverance as a young engineer, in a tiny startup circa 1990. We were anticipating a world with very thin and light multimedia laptops, and so we focused on building a pointing device as a flat and inexpensive touchpad. Our guiding principle was a kind of flat trackball but also with pressure sensitivity so it could "feel" the user. At the time I didn't have an engineering team, so I had to keep plugging away at various aspects, moving from sensor design to manufacturing to analog circuits to microcontrollers to device drivers to demonstration apps.

Every day brought a new problem to tackle resulting in a small advancement that revealed more challenges. I would immerse myself in a particular problem all day, consider known solutions and try to understand their weaknesses, but I wouldn't really try to find the innovation. Then the next day, I would wake up and shower – and boom! The next piece of the puzzle would present itself and I could advance to the next problem. This became a routine.

One early morning, a garbage truck pulled up outside my window and made such a loud racket that it roused me from a deep sleep. Suddenly conscious and sitting up in a daze, I could see all of the terms and ideas that I was working with the previous day, all swirling about looking for places to settle. I can't say if this learning and sleep cycle is a normal brain function for other people, but once I understood what was happening, it made sense to exploit it. I have since used this pattern with engineering teams to get to an invention. What is common to all people is that we need some rest to consider tough problems over time. When a team can challenge each other's ideas, then step back and leave time for deeper reflection, it can be a huge accelerator to the creative thinking process.

Start with Strategy

When innovating, check your motivations. Just because you come up with an invention, or even just an improvement, doesn't mean that it would be useful or that people will want it. Just because you solved a problem, doesn't mean that people will appreciate your solution. Just because you identified a need and creatively built a product that satisfies the need, doesn't mean that there will be enough of a market response to actually build a business. As engineers, we can totally love the brilliant things that we do, but brilliance doesn't always translate into success.

To illustrate, here's an example from my days working on a Network Operating System, circa 1995. I noticed that our company was expending a great effort writing client software for the many types of computers and each desktop operating system and version. An intriguing new tech was just emerging and creating a buzz – the web browser – and with its universal interface that runs on any computer, I thought we could save a ton of money by writing one network client for a web browser and skip a lot of the platform-specific coding. That was an engineer's technology insight, and not a well thought-out product concept. At the time I was studying for an MBA, so I decided to take the business approach out for a whirl and do some market research before going much further with the idea.

That investigation into enterprise pain points and costs revealed that the killer application would be remote email, and not the file transfer feature I originally envisioned. So that's what we did, beating our competitors by a year. As per the business plan that I wrote, this is also a story of market disruption – would customers understand that they could throw away their banks of dial-up servers and long-distance phone accounts? Product reviews were glowing, and customers were writing about how much money they were saving. This was a great result, and only because I was willing to put down my technical concept and look for a worthy problem that was needing to be solved.

It isn't wrong to start off with an engineering inspiration or technical insight, but it is unlikely that the first technical solution you think of will be the one that delivers market success. From time to time an engineer in your company will flash such an idea and they may be very excited about it. They may beg your indulgence, but the best thing you could do for them would be to slow down their technical thinking and pivot them toward business thinking. You can do that by pairing them with a Product Manager, asking the PM to mentor the engineer and get them involved in the investigation to understand potential business drivers. Just handing the engineer a no-go decision from an opaque process will leave them frustrated, but involving them in the business exploration will leave them enriched and better able to make more valuable contributions in the future.

The Inside Entrepreneur

So let's say that you've done your homework and you have a brilliant idea – not just a technical insight, but a business plan and perfect clarity to get to a successful product. Do you need to leave your company for a startup? Maybe not. Established companies need startups, too, because at some point the incremental changes that brought success are not enough to spark innovation, to achieve a jump in growth, to overcome a competitive threat, or to remain relevant in a world of changing technology.

The organizational challenge is that a startup is disruptive by its nature, it's not in the linear path of product evolution that a company has become comfortable with, which is why tech companies rarely articulate the need for their own disruption. They may identify an opportunity to acquire an externally developed product or capability, but that is quite different than realizing the need for an internal opportunity to innovate, and tolerating the risk to pull it off. Maybe your idea can help your company pull its nose up, if only you could get them to see the light.

The following is a set of strategies to help get your idea understood, approved, and funded. But first let's put it out there – a full frontal assault telling people that you have a brilliant idea won't cut it. People have busy lives and aren't expecting you to show up and change their thinking, and you may find the antibodies coming out to attack your foreign concept. Make no mistake, getting internal approval and funding is a selling process to unwitting buyers.

Partner with a Product Manager

A Product Manager can complement your engineer's technical background with business perspective, understanding of customer requests and pain points, relationships to key decision-makers in the company, and knowledge of the company's landscape of roadmaps and plans and budgets. Neglect any of these and you may be blindsided by factors you didn't know exist so you couldn't even make a reasoned defense. If you can't warm up a PM and convince them to work with you, it's not likely that you would get any further, so this is your first test.

Write a Business Plan

First and foremost, you are about to make a huge time and career investment, so write a business plan to convince yourself that it can succeed. The Biz Plan should lead you through a discovery process that exposes different approaches, opportunities, and risks that you hadn't thought of. It's far less costly and easier to test your idea and find its failure modes on paper. Do you think that you already know the market so well that you can skip this step? That would be your first failure, so write a plan. Then it can also become a selling document.

Follow the Process

It's less common, but some companies may actively solicit ideas and provide a standardized process to present them for consideration. This could be a write-up and may even be online, but in the fun cases it could be an ideas fair where you are essentially competing with other aspiring inventors and entrepreneurs. Take any opportunity to showcase your ideas, and after you've been rejected, do it again.

File a Patent Application

Most tech companies will have a process for filing a patent application, sponsored through the legal department's Intellectual Property office. Some engineering organizations have a patent committee that reviews applications before submission, or even actively encourages engineers to submit their ideas. Submitting a patent application not only starts the process for protecting the intellectual property of your novel idea, but gets visibility in the company and may even create a buzz.

Target the Influencers

Very often senior management and any key decision-makers rely on the opinions of a few trusted individuals when it comes to evaluating technology options, market approaches, and new product investments. Ask around and figure out who they are. It may seem efficient to gather everyone in a meeting, make a presentation, and expect them all to fall in love with your idea and throw money at you. They won't. Take your time, approach each influencer one at a time in a private conversation, and allow them to have time to reflect on your idea and give you feedback. Make adjustments and keep going. Then circle back and ask them how they can be helpful to you in bringing your proposal to senior management for consideration and approval. This approach may seem tedious, but a slow success is a better outcome than a fast failure.

Social Networking

Sometimes an idea seems to be "in the air." Lots of people are talking about it casually in meetings or at lunch. "Hey, have you heard about…?" This is extremely powerful because decision-makers may end up hearing about the idea from multiple places, they will be curious about it, or may even think that someone's already working on it. You can make that happen by continually having small-setting conversations and presentations. Be the spark. Like any social message, it will get distorted in retelling, so your job is to play the role of the message police and keep the idea aligned. Then, strike with an implementation proposal when the time feels right.

Skunkworks

If a picture paints a thousand words, a working prototype is priceless for conveying your idea quickly, and making it seem less risky and more realistic than a powerpoint description ever could. Keep it simple, the prototype needs to demonstrate the most important principles and nothing more. Smoke and mirrors are encouraged. If it takes a few people to pull it off, negotiate some set-aside time with your manager. If you and a few helpers aren't willing to put in sweat overtime to make this happen, then do you really believe in the idea?

Do It Anyway

You may get a senior executive to allow your project but not approve it, per se. I once initiated a joint product development with another large software company (it begins with M), where the president of our business unit told me "this is a terrible idea, please don't do it, but I won't stop you." As my internal partner said, "we are so far out on a limb and keep sawing behind us!" We completed the project and launched. When industry analysts started gushing, the president came back to me and said "you were right, I'm glad that you did it." I do not recommend that you commence a startup under these conditions, but here it is.

Present at a Customer Advisory Board

When you don't yet have a product and must be secretive about your idea because it is your company's intellectual property, you can't just go to a conference and blabber to a lot of people about it. A safe place to present to a group of customers and get immediate feedback is a Customer Advisory Board. This is sometimes done when selling into an enterprise market. A CAB might be an annual event and participation is by selected invitation. Attendees expect to hear advanced product information and be part of the process that refines those ideas into real capabilities that could benefit them. Check with a Product Manager if your company manages a CAB.

Get the Sales Team to Validate the Market

This is an extremely effective approach because (1) the sales team actually knows the customers and their needs and you don't, and (2) executives will listen to what the sales team is demanding because they bring in the bucks. Like any population, some 10–15% of a sales team will be forward-looking and interested to have some adventure in order to get a bigger gain. We call them the "hunters" as opposed to the "farmers" that won't help you, so start having conversations with the sales team and figure out who the hunters are. Work with them to target key accounts and go on a few sales calls (you may need to have them sign an NDA) to figure out what customers would really want from your idea. Be prepared to make changes once you get feedback.

Sell One

Again, find a forward-thinking and trusted sales account manager, and target a specific enterprise customer or two where you believe they have a need that is well matched to your idea. Go on a sales call and sell one. Right now you are thinking, "but I haven't built it yet, how can I sell it?" Correct. Talk about taking on a lot of risk. But if it is an important customer that has validated your idea with the intent to purchase, the company decision-makers will need to take notice and probably accept the fate that you must deliver on your idea.

You may be thinking that some of these approaches are crazy and unworkable, but I have literally taken all of the above actions as an *inside entrepreneur*, and nearly all have led to product releases. There is no right way to do it. Look at your situation, take one or more of these approaches as a starting point, and figure out your own path.

Taking an idea from zero to launch is exhilarating, so… go get 'em!

Recap

Innovation requires active and sustained engagement, but it's a process that can be learned and managed. It is important for an innovation manager and team to understand the fundamentals of intellectual property because there are many alternatives, including copyrights, patents, and trade secrets. Open source software has become a well-accepted approach to managing IP, but the details of an open source license must be well understood because it can have a great impact on business.

When an innovative idea springs from a technical insight, it is worth doing market research to make sure your team will be building a product that will be solving a problem that is big enough to drive a successful business outcome. Start with market and product strategy and your innovations will stand a far greater chance of success. As President Eisenhower remarked, "plans are worthless, but planning is everything," so put the effort into writing a business plan.

Being an inside entrepreneur is a valid path to leading innovation, since many established companies need innovation even if they haven't identified the need. Just like a startup there will be many obstacles, but the hardest part is influencing people to adopt your way of disruptive thinking when they have other things on their minds. There are many approaches to go about launching your idea inside a company, while the one that doesn't work is proposing your great idea to decision-makers and assuming that everyone will love it.

CHAPTER 12

Organizational (Mis) Behavior

Organizational Behavior might be one of the first disciplines that an MBA student encounters because it accepts that organizations are first and foremost social systems, and all of the other business topics will be greatly affected by our behaviors in social situations. Truly great companies must be getting a lot of these behaviors right, and achieving massive scale with sustained financial success gives them the right to be confident in their approach.

Nevertheless there must be some exceptions, even at the most successful companies. In some cases, bad decisions or bad policies can be masked by other things going so well. In other cases, everything may be working great, but a single flaw can prove to be tragic. I have had the privilege of working for a bunch of great companies across several industries, and have also had a front seat to observe many spectacular blunders and failures. Pretty much all of the failures that I've seen are the result of our behaviors and decisions, and not being the victim of a terrifying competitor or market threat.

So, a few more things need to be said about managing within a technology company, generally along the lines of things that we do with good intentions that just end up hurting ourselves.

© David J. Asher 2024
D. J. Asher, *Mastering the Complex World of Software Management*,
https://doi.org/10.1007/979-8-8688-0841-8_12

Unscientific Management

Managing is the discipline of getting people to do things in alignment with the stated mission and goals of their organization, usually within the context of paying them to do something that they would otherwise never choose to do on their own. This situation could set up a conflict between the organization's goals and the workers trying to do just enough to get paid. How would we know if we are being effective as managers, making progress against this conflict, or whether we could be making improvements? Let's start with a look back.

The field of Scientific Management started with Frederick Taylor back in the late 19th century, with the objective of improving worker productivity. At the time, "worker" meant manufacturing, and any improvements that could speed up repetitive operations would result in higher productivity, meaning more gets accomplished for each hour worked. Aside: disability benefits and repetitive stress injuries hadn't been invented yet.

Taylor's approach was consistent with the ideals of scientific inquiry. He was experimental and methodical, continuously improving his recommendations based on measurements and analysis. But Taylor wasn't just successful because his approach was scientific; he was studying operations where a worker's actions had a clear and direct relationship to a result, so changes in measurements could be ascribed to changes in a worker's actions with very high confidence.

Now suppose that we've grown weary of guessing and like this idea of Scientific Management, so here in the modern day we would like to improve the productivity of coders. Our first question is, what outcome would we like to measure?

Consider the most impactful result – making money. If your software engineers are producing more, innovative, higher quality code, shouldn't that directly lead to higher sales? That seems like a reasonable relationship to assume; however, along with the variables of code volume and quality that may impact revenue, there are other variables like the performance of other teams contributing to the same project, weaknesses in marketing or sales, customer support experiences, conditions in the economy, competitive strengths, and so on. With so many confounding variables, there's no way to reliably work backwards from an abstract outcome like revenue and understand whether some changes in coding behavior made any impact.

What other measurements relating to code could we use as an outcome metric? Maybe code volume, such as the number of lines of code? If it's more code that you're after, that is easily accomplished: just tie your engineers' compensation to code increases and you'll get more code. It may be buggy and unneeded bloatware, but you'll get a lot of it! You may come up with reasonable proxies for code quality and functionality, such as the customer support caseload, or number of product requirements satisfied. These may be imperfect but would be more directly relatable to a coding team's performance, having fewer confounding variables.

Even if we found some useful metrics representing software development outcomes, how could we identify and test for behavior changes that purport to improve productivity? There could be some technical aspects that are based on time and are easy to quantify. For example, if you have a build process that consumes 30 minutes and optimize it to take only ten minutes, you can simply add up those time savings.

The more interesting factors are behaviors. Take one example – code reviews, and suppose that you're wasting time with all of those reviews and can get better productivity without them. One way to somewhat scientifically test that theory is with a controlled experiment. Ask some teams to stop reviewing code while other teams enforce a complete code review requirement. You can then look at rates such as function points accomplished or bugs released to compare results between teams. You could also investigate this question in a less disruptive way, such as collecting data about the number of coding change suggestions or bugs prevented in your existing code review process.

Things get murkier when you look more broadly than technical coding behaviors and consider policies applied across an organization. Do people perform better when they are allowed to have their pets stay in the office? Are they more productive with a four-day or five-day work week? Do workers improve when getting performance reviews twice a year instead of once? Do we get better hiring results with three interviews or six? You may have theories that explain why some of these options lead to better results, but unless you measure the driving factors and outcomes, and in some cases perform experiments with variations, you should not have confidence that your theories are correct.

And that is the crux of most corporate policies: we don't evaluate them in any systematic way so we just assume that our policies are helpful, but we really don't know. Here's what we do know. When our company is successful, we attribute that success to all of our policies and behaviors – if our outcomes are great, then our processes must be great, all of them. These then become dogma and very difficult to question their effectiveness, much less change. This does not imply that we do things that are counterproductive or that existing policies are bad, we just don't really know if they are good.

Engineering is quite good at taking established practices and repeating them, but it is scientific inquiry that teaches us how to look critically, ask tough questions, reject our assumptions, and develop experiments and analyses to figure out how things really work. It is helpful to have a few scientific thinkers on an engineering team.

The Inhumanity of Tickets

A customer support call comes in, resulting in workflow across several teams until a satisfactory answer can be resolved and returned to the customer. Case closed. The common way to track this workflow to make sure that nothing gets lost is a ticket. A quality team finds a bug and opens a ticket so that a triage, repair, and testing cycle across teams can be completed without losing track. An employee has a problem or question they submit to the HR helpdesk, who opens a ticket to make sure they complete the workflow of resolving the request and responding to the employee.

Before ticketing systems (or, issue trackers) any method such as paper forms or spreadsheets would be slow and error prone. Ticketing systems became essential to many companies precisely because they work so well in these situations. It then wasn't much of a leap for software engineers to notice the similar workflow pattern with coding assignments, especially tasks defined in an Agile backlog, so the use of tickets expands.

Notice how, in each of these examples, a ticket represents work expected and work done, shared among the specific people that need to participate in the workflow. The participants aren't abstractions; they are named people. It was a specific quality engineer that entered a bug, so a development engineer knows who to ask if they require more information than was deposited in the ticket. It was a specific named employee that made an HR helpdesk request, and it is usually a named responder. One of the reasons why these ticketing systems work so well is that they are adjuncts to our human processes and often allow us to interact outside of a ticket when needed, while keeping us safe from forgetting important tasks.

Now suppose that we improve our software build system by including an automated source code quality scanner that looks for known error patterns and reports them back to the originator of the code. We don't want to lose this important quality check that needs to be reviewed and possibly fixed, so our build process generates a ticket. This ticket is just like all of the other bug reports and software development tasks except for one thing – the return address is a machine.

Perhaps our security team has learned of a new critical vulnerability that must be urgently addressed in order to maintain our excellent security posture. It is an imperative that various software development teams must follow the workflow, investigate their code for vulnerability, fix their code, deploy the changes, and report back to the security team. A ticket would be perfect, issued as a high priority work item on each software team's task list.

In these cases where a ticket is issued by a machine, there is no person to whom a software team can reasonably negotiate the priority of acting on this ticket, or to make corrections because the ticket may be in error, or to dig deeper into the problem. There may be someone on the originating team that can handle complaints, but that is different than being the originator of a ticket. These machine-generated ticketing tools can't be perfect, so some of the tickets will be issued falsely in the first place. Can you see where this is going? While most of the machine-generated tickets will just get dispatched routinely, some of them will require person-to-person discussion, and when one half of that relationship is a machine that isn't listening, it can be a very frustrating experience.

Now let's bring Artificial Intelligence into the picture. Since we already have a ticketing tool that can issue work orders to anyone, it's a small jump to have an AI program issuing tickets and starting to control the workflow of people. Perhaps in this case the AI issuer is actually listening and will respond to queries. You may get a useful answer, but sometimes you'll get a hallucination, and most of the time you'll probably get the same kind of responses that we see from automated customer support systems. Oh, the inhumanity.

There is a corollary issue to ticket inhumanity that is worth raising here, which is automated email alerts. It is so easy for a process to alert you that something is starting, and alert you again with progress, and alert you again with status, that your inbox becomes flooded with this noise, rendering it utterly useless. Your defense is to establish inbox filtering rules that deposit the stream to a folder that will never get looked at. What strange behavior.

Hiring Mistakes

One of the most important jobs of any manager, whether you're leading a software development team or you are the CEO, is to get the right people on your team, so it's worth delving into the hiring process. Some of your frustration in hiring great technical and managerial talent may be of your own design, and not too hard to fix. Most of these mistakes are inadvertent, which means that we just haven't been paying enough attention.

Leaving the Funnel Wide Open

You all know how much LinkedIn has positioned itself as the hub of hiring professionals, but even if you're using some other recruiting platforms, it just takes a few clicks for a candidate to submit a job application. The barrier to get to your hiring inbox is almost non-existent. The result is vast resume clutter that makes it extraordinarily difficult to pick the best candidates from a sea of noise. Companies have been addressing this problem with the use of Applicant Tracking Systems that screen resumes and make recommendations based on the job description. Addressing the problem, but not solving it, because the input to your hiring funnel is still too wide and your ATS is really not doing the selective job that you need.

A better way forward is to have each candidate self-select and not even enter your hiring funnel if there isn't a good match. You can accomplish this by asking the candidate just a few thought-provoking open-ended questions on the application form. Any candidate that isn't serious about your job won't take the time and effort to give a reasonable answer.

Don't be thinking that you are giving yourself more material to review, think about how much you have reduced the funnel to a set of serious candidates.

Testing Candidates for Something Else

There are many kinds of tests that job candidates may be subjected to, and some of these, like a coding challenge, may also serve the purpose of narrowing the input funnel. The hiring team just gets the test score and that's an easy hiring filter. Seems like a good idea. What's problematic is that the test being given may not actually align with the hiring goals or the job skills required. That may be easier to see with a coding challenge, where the candidate is asked to perform a coding task that isn't relevant to the team that's hiring. This is common because hiring teams often don't get involved in the coding challenge, they just want to see the passing result; however, this detachment could exclude some candidates that are very strong in other dimensions. This testing mismatch problem gets murkier when it strays into soft skills, general intelligence, and personality evaluations.

Working Against Diversity

Think of a candidate testing process as a selectivity filter that, the more specific and challenging the test is, the narrower the band of candidates that can pass through it. But that isn't just a smaller set; the candidates are also filtered to be more similar. In an age where we have hiring goals for diversity – and hiring teams should appreciate that intellectual diversity and perspective diversity build stronger teams – the testing process can work in opposition to hiring goals. If you are testing for the wrong characteristics, you shouldn't have confidence that your test is improving the quality of job candidates.

Over-specifying the Job Description

You probably don't intend to look for perfection, but by putting every wish-list detail about the ideal candidate on the job description (JD), you may be making it harder on yourself. It would help to take a careful edit cycle of all the job requirements, and just like a good editor, start cutting. Some JDs have so many boiler-plate requirements that it's hard to see what the really important qualification factors are. If a requirement is very generic that any professional candidate would meet it, then don't clutter the JD for the sake of completeness.

Underestimating Candidate Learning Ability

It is also common to see requirements that are overly specific about particular skills or knowledge, such as believing that a programmer knowing one language can't work in another. Hiring managers are often making this contradiction:

- We want to hire the smartest people that can figure things out quickly.

- We want to hire people that already have the skills we need.

Translation: we don't really believe candidates can quickly learn new skills for our job. If you had a choice between a candidate that has demonstrated that they learn new skills quickly, or a candidate that happens to already know the skill but hasn't shown a pattern of picking up new skills, which is the greater long-term benefit for your team? Or maybe your hiring practices are only meeting short-term goals?

Hiding Your Critical Requirement

This is the opposite problem of over-specification. Some JDs may have a lot of detail, and yet still don't express what the hiring threshold is really about. The hiring team should have discussed and aligned on key factors. Screeners and interviewers may leave an interview session believing that the candidate doesn't have the needed experience; however, they may not have been explicit enough in their questions. Giving a general question and hoping the candidate would guess the answer that's in your head isn't fair to both the candidate and the hiring team. If you're looking for an answer about a specific skill or experience, frame the question more specifically. The candidate needs to sell themselves to the interviewer, so they need to know what's important. It's okay to help them understand that.

Ignoring Your Own Candidates

Sometimes the answer is staring you in the face. There is someone on staff that can be transferred or promoted into a new role, but you won't consider that option. We box people in. Everyone gets assigned a compartment, and we think we know all about them, all of their skills, all of their experience, all of their ambitions, and especially all of their constraints. Except those assumptions are almost always insufficient because you simply can't get that deeply into someone else's head.

If you do have someone on staff that believes they are capable of handling more responsibility, but you refuse to ask them, don't be surprised when their enthusiasm drops as the new hire walks in the door. You may have created a new exit by making an outside hire, because you have just insulted someone's career ambitions. The best way to handle these kinds of responsibility promotions is to be prepared and always be thinking about expanding staff and even your own succession. Continually test people with greater challenges, especially getting your team outside of their comfort zone, and with that you can discover which people have the aptitude and inclination to advance.

Down-leveling the Candidate

Here's another contradiction in your JD:

- We want a candidate that is innovative, aggressive, and will seek growth.

- We want a candidate that has already succeeded at a larger role.

Why would you expect this stellar candidate to be attracted to your diminished role? This contradiction comes from a place of avoiding risk. The thinking goes: you can make sure that a candidate will succeed at the new role if they have already proven themselves beyond your job requirements. And at that point you are effectively trying to attract a candidate with a lesser role. Maybe that's acceptable if you are offering them some other exciting new opportunity or significant bump in compensation, but it may also just reflect your own risk aversion.

Ghosting Candidates

Respect is a two-way street, and the first impression that you make with a candidate is your communication during the hiring process. A little bit of honest information about the reasons for the candidate not matching the job requirements could be extremely helpful. Or even just giving them any acknowledgement, and giving it quickly, may be an improvement to your practices. Sometimes a few candidates have completed an interview process and then you face a decision. You want to make an offer to the lead candidate, but don't want to reject the secondary ones because you may need them if the lead candidate rejects their offer. That could leave a considerable amount of time where the secondary candidates have completed the interview and are hearing nothing. It's okay to let them know what's going on.

Building Diverse Teams

Innovation most often happens, not from a completely novel concept, but from an inspired connection between previously unrelated ideas. When everyone on a team is drawn from the same pool of engineers experienced in the same domain, it is less likely that a tough problem will be solved by making a cognitive connection with a foreign idea. So it should not come as a surprise that I have observed the most innovative and high-performing teams to be built on diversity: intellectual diversity, academic diversity, diversity of perspective, and diversity of technical domain experience.

As I write this, the United States is in the midst of a raging argument about Diversity, Equity, and Inclusion (DEI) programs in college campuses and across corporate America. Because these programs are influencing hiring practices at the corporate level, they are having an impact on software teams and how they are built. The intended influence in the hiring process is to broaden identity diversity, but does not pay attention to the other important kinds of diversity that are truly critical when building innovative and highly productive teams.

Here is my hiring experience: if you have a hiring process that tries to remove bias and focuses on intellectual, academic, perspective, and domain diversity, then identity diversity should be an outcome. If identity diversity is an input constraint, you will probably suffer in the other diversity types.

You may find that you have certain corporate-level restrictions placed on your hiring practices, so for a moment please follow me on a thought experiment where you are completely free to establish the hiring practices that are best suited for your own team. The first step would be to remove bias in the front-end hiring filter. To do this, you could have someone sanitize the set of submitted resumes by removing each candidate's name, any location information, the names of the schools they attended, any experiences earlier than 10 or 15 years prior, and any indicators of disabilities. You could perform this same kind of identity masking when presenting the hiring team with results from a coding challenge or other tests. Then the hiring team can review these candidates as an essentially unbiased view of the input funnel. It is difficult to remove bias from the interview and evaluation process, but anti-biasing can be reinforced by continually discussing diversity factors in the decision process. And now, back to the real world.

Designed to Fail

It seems that most tech companies are short-lived. Why do so few achieve long-term traction, and can we do better? My hypothesis is that we design tech companies to fail, and somehow just a few make it past the hurdles that we create.

First, let's consider the special case of monopolies. Look at this string of persistent tech titans: IBM, Intel, Microsoft, Oracle, Google, Amazon, Apple... what they share is being founded on an organizing principle so strong that they could parley it to near monopoly power. Once a monopoly, they can make all sorts of costly and terrible blunders and yet not endanger their core business cash machine. Monopolizing companies are an exception to any rational way of operating a business, and their behaviors and business practices may not be too helpful as examples for the rest of us that don't have monopoly power. When looking to emulate any behaviors of a monopolizing company that you might admire, start with critical analysis and don't believe your own wishful thinking.

There are so many ways to fail. For a tech company to thrive, it needs to be defensive against failure modes as well as having a successful strategy. Here are a few of them:

- Not pivoting the core product to a new competitive offering when under existential threat from market changes and technology advancements; often this is caused by a cultural denial or complacency that prevents reacting to market pressure.

- Starving a cash cow business, assuming that it will continue to throw off profits even without vigorous investment and innovation.

- Chasing big bet product alternatives in order to break out from the cash cow into a major second act, only lightly vetting a business case under the assumption that big rewards demand bid risks and misunderstanding that poorly managed risks often lead to failure.

- Ignoring competitive threats because competitive analyses aren't performed or because responding to threats would demand risky decisions and uncomfortable changes.

- Acquiring a struggling company that makes unrealistic claims, or that will distract critical resources from successful programs, likely because inadequate due diligence was done.

- Failing to effectively market a product that was successfully developed and had exciting market potential, forcing a loss of return on investment.

- Failing to develop a product strategy because today's linear thinking doesn't allow for considering tomorrow's needed change, or worse, paying huge amounts to a consultant to give you a strategy when creating a strategy is your job.

- "This is a strategic program": any time you hear an executive claim a program is strategic, this is a key word that translates to a decision on a gut instinct without a business case; just run away.

- Launching new products into non-adjacent markets that demand opening new channels to customers, which is one of the hardest and riskiest business pivots.

- Outsourcing development to lower costs while not appreciating the intellectual property contributions of key developers.

- Tolerating mediocrity in top leadership positions.

- Tolerating toxic programs that are sucking up resources and already determined not to be worthy of continued investment, but somehow keep getting funded.

- Ignoring risk factors when making a critical business decision to fund a shiny new thing because the shininess of the shiny new thing is so blinding.

- Ignoring non-customers, the ones who already refused to buy your product and that hold the keys to market growth if you would just look at their reasoning.

- Not knowing your place on the technology adoption cycle, since product and market strategy need to shift in different ways depending on your product's phase in the cycle.

- Failing to put attention to scaling challenges when growing because all systems, whether it's an architecture or database or development team, will stress and then break when subjected to scaling pressure.

- Misunderstanding pricing, and too often tech companies ignore the subtleties of how pricing strategy will impact the sales cycle, customer relationships, competitive positioning, and accounting consequences.

- Insufficient paranoia, or overconfidence, in market position.

You may know more. These are just some of the failures that I've witnessed first-hand and up close. It's painful to watch, especially when the failure outcomes are predictable. So how do tech companies, with such fantastic resources of really smart and driven people, get into failure modes? Here are a few ways.

Untrained Management

Some industries are attentive to the complexities of business management and people management, and invest in career advancement by funding employees to enter programs such as an MBA or have developed internal training that purposefully builds up people to become competent managers. Not so much for tech companies. Many engineering leaders without business training seem to disdain people with an MBA, not really appreciating what they themselves don't know. When looking for management and executive talent, they often look to hire from the outside, because they don't see the management talent that they need within their ranks, because they didn't attempt to develop that talent. A growing tech company is moving fast and is too focused on technology to concern themselves with training people and career development, not when you can just buy talent from someone else.

Governance by Inertia

What corporate structure and governance is very good at is doing the same thing over and over again. This is beneficial and highly efficient most of the time, but fails us when change is really required. As companies enjoy success and grow, their set of processes and behaviors start to solidify. People get hired with specific roles to play, and they play them. Culture forms, executives make policies, HR sets rules, and managers hold their teams accountable for these. Customers have incremental demands that must be delivered. The sales team applies pressure to act only in the satisfaction of a 90-day window. Code gets big and messy and tech debt accrues and it's hard to escape the mistakes in product architecture. Workers are rewarded for hitting executive-approved goals that may diverge over time from decisions that would really lead to growth and profitability and social good, but hey, you can't miss your goals. Basically, everyone on the team is playing defense.

Spot the Problem

Let's say that you are a keen observer and notice your company is doing things that will lead to stagnation or failure. What then? Are you going to explain to HR that their rules are harmful? That your VP has set counterproductive goals? That your manager is ignoring tech debt that will explode into a crisis? That the CEO just approved an acquisition that any half-technologist can see is a dud or a fraud? That investment in a brilliant new business will starve the cash cow and bring the whole thing down? That the CIO is forcing the use of tools that are hurting your ability to compete? And even if you do have such a keen understanding of the problem, where's your evidence, can you prove that keeping the status quo will result in failure? It's just you spouting your opinion against the rest of the company that is doing just fine, thank you. The result is that organizations have an automatic rejection of change ideas until a crisis happens.

Downside and Upside

Step back a moment, and you may appreciate that none of the entrenched parties in a company actually has an interest in hearing your complaint or doing anything about it. The things that worked today should still work for another day, but making a disruptive change could risk breaking all sorts of things and require a whole lot of work. The CEO has a parachute and plenty of people to blame if things go wrong. The executives will get new jobs by spinning a story that it was someone else's failure that created a bad situation. There's little downside when avoiding a risky change for executives in the corporate hierarchy. The upside of making a risky change is what, a reward that hasn't been defined, to prevent a failure that no one is anticipating? By design, a manager in the hierarchy has every incentive to avoid change, even if avoiding change carries a huge risk of its own. Any risks of inaction are defensible, but the risk of making a change decision could be real accountability.

Change Agent

You see an existential problem, so what can you do? You can be quiet, or be an irritant; there is no in-between. From the perspective of managers in the hierarchy, it's not just threatening their way of doing business and the familiar routines of their jobs, but in their minds, changing the status quo threatens their livelihoods. Which is why you will most probably stay quiet when you see failure modes happening before your eyes, or maybe just grumble on Slack. In a bureaucracy, one person shouting about a deep problem isn't a prophet, they are a madman.

Which all helps to explain why so many frustrated people in a tech company leave their employer for another company with a better story. Or at least a different story and different culture, or that is so shiny and hasn't shown its failure modes yet. Job switching costs are low in the tech industry so it's little problem to get away from the inertia that's irritating you and maybe make a little more money. Or if you're really looking for adventure, leave for a startup and begin the cycle anew.

Recap

Taking a social perspective of an organization can yield many insights revealing how much our behaviors can work against our own best interests. The policies and decisions made by managers and executives often aren't validated with measurements and feedback. While it would be exhausting to apply this kind of rigor universally, we rarely take care to confirm the benefits or drawbacks of the most important and impactful policies. For most tech companies, our policies are running open-loop.

Sometimes the information technologies that we use to make our tasks more efficient end up creating new kinds of problems. One example is ticketing systems that start out as a means to keep track of information between human interactions, but can become oppressive when one-half of the parties is a machine. Another example is auto-generated email that submerges our inboxes with a flood of useless messages.

With the bedrock of success depending on the people who are hired for our teams, our hiring practices are critical. There are many actions that we take in the hiring process that actually make our jobs harder or less likely to find the best candidates. If it's innovation that you're after, and for many other reasons, the best approach is building diverse teams. If you try to unbias your process and focus on intellectual diversity, academic diversity, diversity of perspective, and diversity of technical domain experience, then identity diversity will follow.

It is very hard work to get a technology company to startup and grow but even so many are able to achieve it. What is less common is longevity. Sustaining success over the long run is very rare, and if we step back and wonder why that is, we can find many structural causes that seem to conspire to bring down a successful company. It even looks like tech companies are designed to fail over the long team.

CHAPTER 13

Coda

Artificial Intelligence is already having a significant impact on software development, so we would be basking in our own hubris to think that it won't impact management. I didn't have to wonder how, since ChatGPT was more than willing to give me the answer.

Me:

ChatGPT, please describe how artificial intelligence will replace the role of a software development manager.

ChatGPT:

Artificial intelligence (AI) has the potential to significantly impact the role of a software development manager in several ways:

1. **Automated Project Management:** AI can automate many project management tasks traditionally performed by a software development manager. This includes scheduling, resource allocation, progress tracking, and risk management. AI-driven project management tools can analyze data to predict project outcomes, identify potential bottlenecks, and suggest optimized strategies.

© David J. Asher 2024
D. J. Asher, *Mastering the Complex World of Software Management*,
https://doi.org/10.1007/979-8-8688-0841-8_13

2. **Code Generation and Analysis:** AI-powered tools can generate code based on specifications, reducing the need for manual coding by developers. Additionally, AI can analyze code for bugs, vulnerabilities, and adherence to coding standards. This reduces the burden on development managers to manually review code and ensures higher quality software releases.

3. **Team Collaboration and Communication:** AI-driven collaboration platforms can facilitate communication and coordination among team members. These platforms can analyze communication patterns, identify potential conflicts or misunderstandings, and suggest strategies for improving team dynamics. Development managers can leverage these insights to foster a more productive and cohesive team environment.

4. **Resource Optimization:** AI can analyze data on developer performance, project requirements, and resource availability to optimize team composition and workload distribution. This ensures that projects are staffed appropriately and that developers are allocated to tasks that align with their skills and expertise.

5. **Predictive Analytics:** AI can analyze historical project data to identify patterns and trends that can inform decision-making. For example, AI algorithms can predict project delivery timelines, budget requirements, and resource needs based on past performance data. Development managers can use these insights to make more informed decisions and mitigate risks.

6. **Continuous Improvement:** AI can facilitate continuous improvement initiatives by analyzing data on software development processes and identifying areas for optimization. This includes identifying inefficient workflows, recommending

process changes, and monitoring the impact of interventions over time. Development managers can use AI-driven insights to drive ongoing improvements in team performance and productivity.

Overall, while AI has the potential to automate many tasks traditionally performed by software development managers, it is unlikely to completely replace the role. Instead, AI will augment the role by automating routine tasks, providing valuable insights, and enabling development managers to focus on higher-level strategic activities such as innovation, team leadership, and stakeholder engagement.

"Unlikely to completely replace the role?" It would say that, wouldn't it?

Index

© David J. Asher 2024
D. J. Asher, *Mastering the Complex World of Software Management*,
https://doi.org/10.1007/979-8-8688-0841-8

GPSR Compliance
The European Union's (EU) General Product Safety Regulation (GPSR) is a set
of rules that requires consumer products to be safe and our obligations to
ensure this.

If you have any concerns about our products, you can contact us on

ProductSafety@springernature.com

In case Publisher is established outside the EU, the EU authorized
representative is:

Springer Nature Customer Service Center GmbH
Europaplatz 3
69115 Heidelberg, Germany

www.ingramcontent.com/pod-product-compliance
Lightning Source LLC
LaVergne TN
LVHW051638050326
832903LV00022B/798